The Pocket Scroll® Series

SHAAR PRESS

# COURAGE

## RABBI ZELIG PLISKIN

# Formulas, stories and insights

*published by*

ARTSCROLL

SHAAR PRESS

# TABLE OF CONTENTS

# INTRODUCTION

We all want and need courage. Courage is a decision to transcend one's fears. It is a quality that enables us to speak up and to take action even though we find it difficult. At times we need courage to remain silent or to refrain from taking action. A lack of courage is one of the greatest handicaps an individual can have.

This is not a book that will train you to become a lion-tamer, a racing-car driver, or a climber of Mount Everest. The courage this book focuses on is the kind we have need of daily: the courage to accomplish and overcome limitations, the courage to make inquiries and requests, the courage to begin and to begin again, and the courage to cope well with all forms of difficulties, challenges, and adversity. Courage is an attribute that will give you an overall sense of strength and well-being.

The importance of courage can be found at the beginning of The Code of Jewish Law (*Shulchan Aruch*). There it is stated that we should not allow the fear of others mocking us prevent us from serving the A-mighty. The fact that this is placed in the very first passage is an indication of just how vital it is to develop this attribute. We need courage not to hesitate and come to a standstill due to fear of disapproval.

New life challenges frequently arise: hardships, illness, financial difficulties, changes in life circumstances, setbacks, unforeseen events. Additional courage is needed to cope with the new tests that arise.

Courage is the quality of great people. More accurately it is a quality that creates greatness. It is the quality of Abraham who recognized the Creator and was willing to give his life in defense of this awareness. It is the quality of Moses who approached Pharaoh and told him, "Let my people go." It is the quality of the righteous Mordechai who refused to bow to the wicked Haman; and of Esther who approached King Ahasuerus on behalf of her people even though she was putting her life at risk. It is the quality of the Jewish people throughout the ages who were willing to sacrifice everything to live a Torah life. It is the quality that will elevate and empower you throughout your existence.

As you read and reread this book, may you be blessed with ever-increasing courage.

I wish to express my deep gratitude to Rabbi Noah Weinberg, Rosh HaYeshivah of Aish HaTorah. His courage has provided inspiration to many.

Once again I express my appreciation to Rabbi Kalman Packouz for his insights and encouragement.

# 1.

# EVERYONE NEEDS MORE COURAGE

*Lack of courage has limited me and caused me great suffering. As a young child I remember how afraid I was to try anything new. Starting school was a nightmare for me. Teachers and other authority figures constantly intimidated me. I was extremely nervous before each test, and this stress prevented me from doing my best.*

*I lived in fear of car accidents every time our family drove anywhere. When we went to the zoo, I was afraid that I would get lost and wouldn't be able to find my parents. When I went somewhere with my father, I worried what I would do in the event he suffered a heart attack. I worried about nuclear war from the time I was 8. I worried about how I would earn a living when I grew up. And the older I got, the more powerful this worry became.*

*In general, I was afraid to speak up and ask for what I wanted. As an adult, the thought of marriage and taking responsibility terrified me. I pushed off getting married for as long as I could. I was extremely anxious about how I would manage with my own children.*

*As I got older and overcame past fears, new ones would spring up.*

*Some people told me that I enjoyed being frightened. That's ridiculous. I hated these feelings. It was just that I didn't know what I could do to overcome them. I considered it my nature to be frightened. I avoided taking any risk that I possibly could. I would always choose the safest path even though it was not the path that would enable me to accomplish as much as I potentially could.*

*I look back at my life with regret. Fear has caused me indescribable misery.*

Imagine how much better this person's life would have been if he had been more courageous. He did evidence sparks of courage now and then. He married. He had a family. He did have a job. But he suffered needlessly. Courage would have alleviated much of that suffering. He did not accomplish a fraction of what he could have if he had had greater levels of courage.

Some people have less courage than this individual. They suffer more and they accomplish even less. They need to increase their level of courage like a starving person needs basic food and water.

Others have high levels of courage in many areas of their lives. But they would still benefit by developing additional courage in specific areas. Some highly successful businessmen who can negotiate with powerful mediators lack the courage to speak publicly. Some people who are unafraid of physical dangers fear that people will laugh at them if they deepen their religious commitment. Some brilliant people are afraid that others may think they are stupid if they ask for clarification when they fail to clearly understand something.

Some people reach middle age with enough courage to have sustained them until that time. At that point they are faced with unforeseen hardships and suffering. They now need more courage than they ever had before.

Some people lack the courage to admit mistakes or faults, to admit that they were wrong or lack knowledge. Some lack the courage to ask for forgiveness. Others lack the courage to tell others not to listen to gossip or speak negatively of others. There are those who lack the courage to acknowledge their vulnerability or their inner feelings. Yet others lack the courage to solicit funds for a worthy cause. Many lack the courage to acknowledge that they lack courage.

The good news is that courage is a trait. Like every trait it can be improved. No one is born with highly developed courage. We are all born as helpless infants. Regardless of how little or how much courage one presently has, there is an ongoing need to gain even more and everyone can learn how to accomplish this.

The very fact you are reading a book on courage is a major step in self-empowerment. As you gain additional courage yourself, you will be able to encourage others throughout your life.

*I always thought that I was a courageous person. I took many risks* and wasn't afraid of doing dangerous things. But I took a son of mine to a lecture on courage because I thought it would benefit him. When I heard the many examples of courage that were brought up by the speaker and other members of the audience, I realized that I had a fear of asking questions in public. I realized that I was afraid to admit that I had any faults. Several people had mentioned this to me before, but I had discounted it. Going home I shared with my son, "I gained more than I thought I would. I realized that I need to increase my own level of courage." This is not something that I could have said previously. My son smiled a great big smile, and said, "Dad, what you just told me was more helpful to me than the entire lecture."

# 2.

# WHAT IS COURAGE?

Courage comes in many flavors. In general, courage is defined as the mental or moral strength to venture, persevere, and withstand danger, fear, or adversity. It is staunchness of mind and of will. It is the strength to face opposition and not allow it to stop you. It is the strength to cope with hardship. It is maintaining your dignity when it is difficult to do so. Courage gives you the empowerment of steely determination. It enables you to strive toward noble aspirations.

There are definitely acts that everyone would consider acts of courage. Take, for example, the person who runs into a burning building to save a young child's life. Or, the person who donates one of his kidneys to save a life thereby putting himself at risk.

When I think of an act of courage, I think of an aunt of mine who was in the concentration camp in Auschwitz. One of her sisters was physically weak and was sent to the line leading to the gas chambers. My aunt managed to get the Nazi officer to look the other way for a moment. She then ran over and with one hand pulled her sister back to the line of life, and with her other hand she pulled the stranger who was next in line. Her daughter learned of this in Macy's in New York many years later. The woman who was saved recognized my aunt and screamed and fainted. My aunt did not recognize the woman. After reviving, the woman said, "I will never forget you. You saved my life."

There is the courage to deal with major financial loss. When the stock market crashed in 1929 there were many who lost their entire fortunes and felt too discouraged to persevere in face of the new challenges in their lives. Courage would have enabled them to cope and continue living as did those who were able to say, "Losing money is painful. But I still have my health and can begin again."

There is the courage to deal with major illnesses and injuries. Included here is the courage to grow from all forms of handicaps. Some people are born with handicaps and others are challenged later in life. Either way, many acts of courage are required to live life to its fullest and not to surrender to defeat.

There is the courage to open a new school, start a new organization, or a new business venture when one lacks any assurance that it will be successful.

There is the courage to take risks to make peace and help resolve disputes. And there is the courage to realize that any efforts on your part could make the situation worse, so you would do better to step aside.

There is the courage to do things that most others are afraid to do, but nonetheless must be done. Every time you willingly do one of those things, you become a more courageous person.

Courage is subjective and relative. For example, some people are naturally assertive. They can readily speak up. They can easily ask others for things. They can comfortably ask questions. They can comfortably stick up for their rights. Others are naturally intimidated. They would rather do without than say even those things that everyone would agree they have a right to say. For them asking for what they need is an act of courage. Asking questions is an act of courage. Sticking up for their rights is an act of courage.

Courageous acts build your character. At times one courageous act can make a hero out of someone. A terrorist threatens to kill as many as he can. One person jumps him and takes away his weapon. That person is changed for life. He will now view himself as a courageous person.

At times one can only recognize courage after having done many acts of courage over a long period of time. People who see this person do not realize the courage he needs to continue to do all that he is doing. This is the courage of many survivors of World War II who lost their entire families and had to start a new life. This is the courage of someone who suffers from chronic physical pain and with supreme effort continues on with life. This is the courage of someone with a serious learning disability who does not let it prevent him from being as scholarly as he is able. This is the courage of someone who continually befriends the friendless. This is the courage that many people manifest in diverse ways. You are likely to encounter these people without realizing it. Thinking about the various ways that one can be courageous will enable you to recognize courage that you previously overlooked. And, either in the present or future, this courageous individual could be you.

Courage is what the Code of Jewish Law (*Shulchan Aruch* 1:1) asks of us when it states that we should not allow fear of being ridiculed hinder our serving the A-mighty.

There are many instances when we will lack the ability to control a situation. Some people feel strong when they feel in control. But they feel overwhelmed when they cannot control events. You always have the ability to control your mental attitude. Courage enables you to maintain an inner sense of empowerment even when you lack the power to control external events.

Throughout your life you will discover more and more definitions of courage. As you reflect on courage and are determined to live with this empowering attribute, your unwritten autobiography will give you greater insight into what it means to have courage.

*The concept of being courageous always fascinated me; at the same time, it made me feel frustrated. "What exactly is courage?" I would ask myself. Since I didn't have a clear definition, it was difficult for me to decide whether or not I was courageous. Somehow this seemed so lofty to me that I often felt it was beyond me.*

*I consulted someone who seemed to me to personify courage. "The first step is to clarify what you would consider the essential components of courage," I was told. "Don't ask others for their definitions. Clarify your own. Picture in your mind what a courageous person would be like. Don't think in terms of the ultimate superhero. Rather, think of courage as an attribute that is attainable by all. What are the inner thoughts of a person with courage? What would differentiate between a person with courage and that same person without it? Be concise and clear."*

*This proved extremely helpful for me, and I have passed this assignment onto others. I've come to realize that we each have our own definition of courage. Those who write down their ideal picture and view it as their personal goal will find themselves making progress.*

# 3.

# DESCENDANTS OF ABRAHAM

"**A**braham, our father, was tested with ten challenges, and he withstood them all" (*Ethics of the Fathers* 5:4).

The ten tests withstood by Abraham are his spiritual legacy. They are gifts to his biological descendants and to all who choose to become his spiritual descendants. His passing the ultimate difficult tests made it easier for us to pass the tests the A-mighty sends our way.

The life history of Abraham is a biography of courage. Abraham recognized the Divine Creator and was willing to sacrifice his life for his beliefs. His father, Terach, owned an idol shop. Abraham as a child bravely smashed the idols. When questioned about what happened, he cleverly told his father that the biggest one smashed the smaller ones. His father could not accept his excuse. And that is exactly how Abraham challenged his father, "If you don't believe the biggest idol could do such a simple task, how can you claim to believe that it has any other power?" Abraham devoted his life to serving the Creator and was willing to face martyrdom at the hands of Nimrod, the powerful leader of the time, rather than renounce the Oneness of G-d. Many of his descendants made similar courageous choices. Abraham was the pioneer who paved the way.

Abraham left his father's home and birthplace in order to follow the wishes of the A-mighty. He willingly faced the unknown. His destination was wherever G-d would tell him to go. His courage was implanted in the spiritual genes of his children for all generations.

When the land where Abraham was told to settle had a famine, he accepted the A-mighty's will and went into exile where he faced a conflict with hostile kings. "No complaints," was Abraham's leitmotif. I personally grew up with a father who echoed this motto. When as a result of cancer my father's health deteriorated, he would say, "No complaints. I'm still alive." And as he told me, "Whenever the A-mighty wants me, I'm ready to go. But we have a commandment to live as long as we can until then."

As a sign of his covenant with G-d, Abraham at an advanced age was willing to undergo a painful initiation. This, too, he did willingly. His love for the Creator transcended any fear of pain.

Isaac, Abraham's son, was precious to his father. This went beyond the usual love of a father for his child; Isaac was the one who would carry on Abraham's life mission. He was the next link in the eternal chain that would forge a special nation devoted to the service of the Creator. When the A-mighty told Abraham to sacrifice his beloved son, Abraham immediately agreed to fulfill His will.

The *Mishnah* which discusses Abraham's passing the ten tests notes that he was "our father." Imagine the power you will feel when you internalize this message. "My father, Abraham, was the ultimate in courage. I have this courage stored within me. It is my right, my obligation, and my privilege to access this whenever I need it." Allow these words to reverberate in your mind and experience the empowerment that they will provide.

Each time you mention Abraham's name in the prayers, you access a reminder of the courage you inherited. Each time you read Abraham's name in the Torah, you have a reminder of the courage you inherited. Each time you meet someone named Abraham, you have yet another reminder of the courage you inherited.

*I knew about Abraham, the father of our people, from the time I was a child. But this was an abstract concept for me. There were some illustrious scholars in my ancestry and I was proud of them as I grew up. But they lived more recently. I recall the day when I read in Rabbi Chaim of Volozhin's book* Ruach Chaim *that each descendant of Abraham personally inherited the ability to pass tests that were similar to Abraham's. I was facing a number of personal difficulties at the time. I felt like I was drowning. The courage I gained from realizing my intrinsic strength enabled me to swim safely through the stormy waters. It took quite a while until my problems were solved, but my newly found courage enabled me to muster the endurance I needed.*

*I am a convert to Judaism. To say that my family didn't approve of this would be an extreme understatement. I didn't have money or relatives when my family disowned me. What kept giving me strength was the knowledge that I was a child of Abraham. I felt his encouragement accompanying me wherever I found myself.*

# 4.

# "WHY AM I SUCH A WIMP?"

*"Why am I such a wimp that I keep pushing off visiting the dentist even though I need to take care of my teeth?"*

*"Why am I such a wimp that I keep saying yes to requests when I should really say no?"*

*"Why am I such a wimp that I don't state my opinion when I disagree with what people say?"*

*"Why am I such a wimp that I let people overcharge me instead of respectfully sticking up for my rights?"*

There is a problem with the questions these people are asking. The questions all lead their askers in the wrong direction. The question they really want answers to is, "What can I do to get the courage I want and need?"

*"What can I do to have the courage to visit the dentist?"*

*"What can I do to have the courage to say, 'No,' when I feel it would*

*create too big of a hardship if I were to say, 'Yes'?"*

*"What can I do to have the courage to state my opinions when I disagree?"*

*"What can I do to have the courage not to allow people to overcharge me?"*

If someone tries to answer a "Why am I such a wimp?" question, he is accepting the premise that he is a wimp. Then he wants to know the cause and root. Maybe he is a wimp because of his genes. Maybe he is a wimp because of his parents being too tough or too weak. Maybe he is a wimp because of his siblings. Maybe he is a wimp because of his environment. Even if he finds out why he is such a wimp, he will still remain one.

A much wiser direction to go is in the direction that will enable us to reach our actual goal: Courage.

Focus on gaining additional courage. Focus on the integration of the beliefs and concepts that create courage. Focus on the behaviors that increase courage. Focus on learning from teachers and coaches who build your courage. Focus on reading articles and books that will help you increase your courage.

After you master courage, you can seek answers, "Why was I such a wimp?" But you may prefer to spend more time on answering, "What can I keep on doing to increase my courage level even more?" Or, "How can I share what I know about courage with others?"

# 5.

# REMEMBERING YOUR MOMENTS OF COURAGE

Every person alive will have memories of saying or doing something that took courage. And every person alive will have memories of when he lacked courage. Remember your best moments and build on them.

When we are faced with a given situation, we can choose to act in a new way. We can choose to speak in a way we have never spoken before. But what is most common is that we follow familiar patterns. Since we all have patterns of courage and patterns of the opposite, the patterns that are uppermost in our minds are the most likely to be repeated. Make it a high priority to remember your best moments. These then serve as a template for how you will act in your present moments.

"But what if I have one hundred clear memories when I lacked courage and only five clear memories when I acted with courage? Won't it be easier for me to recall those one hundred memories?" some people ask.

"Yes," is the answer. "But it is irrelevant."

"I beg to differ. It seems to me to be very relevant," one can easily argue.

"Since you can choose which memory to focus on, you can take even a single incident and mentally repeat it over and over again. Therefore even if you have many more memories of not speaking and acting with courage, you still have the ability to repeatedly access your memories of courage."

This fact that the brain has the ability to recall memories is impossible to argue with. (Well, one can argue with anything. But one who does this time is incorrect.) Let us suppose someone was born and grew up in New York, or in London, or in Paris. He lived in the city of his birth for many years. Then he visited the Western Wall in Jerusalem. He has now seen it just once. The New Yorker has seen the Statue of Liberty hundreds of times. The Londoner has seen Buckingham Palace hundreds of times. The Parisian has seen the Eiffel Tower hundred of times. If you would tell each person after he returns to his hometown, "In your mind, see the Western Wall," he would be able to do it quite easily. Even thought he had seen either the Statue of Liberty, Buckingham Palace, or the Eiffel Tower many more times, his brain will access the pictures of the Western Wall. A person can choose on his own to mentally revisit the Western Wall as often as he wants.

The same applies to each memory in your vast mental library. You can ask your brain to revisit any memory and if that memory was notable it will come to the forefront of your consciousness. This is a most powerful tool for increasing courage.

Your memories of courage have the power to give you courage in the here and now. Let them do their job. Call upon them as often as needed. They will appreciate being remembered and they will enable you to add many new memories of courage to your collection.

*When I was in elementary school, I once asked a question in class and I was laughed at. Thereafter every time I felt like asking a question in the future, that memory came to the forefront of my mind, and I was afraid to ask the question I just thought of. This lasted for many years. Then someone asked me, "Did you ever ask a question and felt good about asking it?"*

*"A few times," I replied. "But what I usually remember are the times when I was laughed at and the times that I was too afraid to ask."*

*"From now on, mentally keep replaying the times that you did ask questions and felt good about asking them. Repeat those memories many times. Since you are running them in your mind, in just a short time you can review those memories many times."*

*Even after I heard this I didn't implement it right away. But over the period of a couple of months I repeated these pictures hundreds of times. To my surprise I spontaneously found myself asking questions in class without any effort.*

*A great scholar and leader visited our city. I usually feel intimidated by authority figures, but I heard that he was accessible. I said to myself, "This is an opportunity that I don't want to miss." I went to discuss a number of issues with him. The fact that this was a rare opportunity gave me the courage to approach him. This memory has given me the ability to approach other authority figures. None of them are of the first scholar's stature and since I was able to take the initiative to speak to him, all the more so I could do the same with others who are not as brilliant and elevated.*

*Again and again I avoided confronting those who appear frightening to me, people with very serious and judgmental looks on their face. I found it easy to confront people who had softer personalities. But I had an abundance of memories of lacking courage. Gentle people brought forth memories of my interacting well with other gentle people. But intimidating faces in the present created a catalogue of instances when I felt frozen.*

*I was told to remember an instance of courage involving these types of people. I did. It was when I insisted that someone who sold me a defective car return my money. That was difficult for me. But the amount of money involved fueled my courage. I firmly persisted even though the salesman tried every tactic he knew to intimidate me. I persisted and eventually he returned my money rather than face the prospect of a lawsuit. From then on that was the memory I called up whenever I was in a similar situation. I still have more memories of being intimidated. But the number of memories in my courage list keeps increasing.*

# 6.

# FOCUS ON PROGRESS

When working on courage, you have a choice. You can picture perfect courage. That is, having total courage all the time in all situations. Less than this is unacceptable. The problem with this choice is that it is likely to create feelings of failure and discouragement. This goal of complete perfection is unlikely to be attained. If you view it as either-or, either I am totally perfect in this trait or I still lack it, you can feel that you totally lack courage even when you are making considerable progress.

Or you can choose to focus on the progress you are making. You have infinitely more courage now than you did when you were born. Since each courageous act makes you a more courageous person, by focusing on progress, you will almost always feel that you are increasing your level of courage. This perspective will give you the encouragement to continue developing this quality. Even if you feel that you are backsliding, you still have made progress from the place where you were when you started your journey in life.

I would strongly recommend that you choose the second pattern. With the first pattern one will continuously be thinking about one's lack of courage. With the second pattern you will be thinking about the increased courage that you have accessed. This will motivate you to continuously grow and improve. What you focus on will become stronger, and you will consistently be focusing on increasing words and deeds of courage.

*I have two friends. Both of them are very conscious of their level of courage. But whenever they experience any fear, they react in totally opposite ways. One will say, "Oh no. I see that I am still afraid of things. I'm afraid that I will always be a coward."*

*The other one responds to his fears, "This is terrific. I have yet another opportunity to make progress. As soon as I am less afraid than I used to be, I will see that I am improving. While I would love to overcome all of my fear completely once and for all, I know that this isn't realistic. The progress I keep making gives my life a sense of achievement."*

*There isn't a major difference in the level of courage of these two fellows. But one is always complaining that he lacks courage. And the other is grateful that he is continually increasing his level of courage.*

# 7.

# FOR THE GOOD

There is a basic Torah concept that will totally transform one's perception of reality. As you internalize and integrate this awareness, you will live a joyous life. This concept will free you from much stress and tension, anger and frustration. And as you view the world from this perspective your level of courage will increase in all areas of your life.

"All that the Almighty does is for the good," is the way Rabbi Akiva put it. And he learned this message from his teacher Nachum, who was called *Ish Gam Zu;* that is, the man who always said, "*Gam zu l'tovah,* This, too, is for the good."

When good things happen in your life, you are happy. And only good things happen. "Good" in this context is that in the entire picture of your life what happens is exactly what you need to happen for your ultimate benefit. When you know for certain that things will work out all right, you are free from much stress and tension. And things always work out the way that they are supposed to. When you know that you will be successful, you have the courage to say and do what needs to be said and done. You choose your actions. The outcome depends on the will of our loving Father and powerful King. And that outcome, whatever it is, is exactly what you need to fulfill your life's mission.

Each day in the prayers we reiterate the *Shema Yisrael*. There we recite the Torah verse that states our obligation to internalize our love for G-d to such an extent that we sustain this even when He takes our soul. Our goal in life is to have a comprehensive awareness that all He does for us throughout our lives is entirely for our ultimate benefit. Therefore we can readily accept the exact details of how our life unfolds. Our life task is to serve our Creator in the settings that He chooses. We can make plans, but His plans are what will actually occur.

The courage that this gave the sage Nachum was incredible. He was blind in both eyes, he was missing both hands and both feet, and his entire body was covered with boils. Added to all this he lived in dire poverty. When others said to him, "Woe to us that we see you like this," he replied, "Woe to me if you would not have seen me like this." The Talmud (*Taanis* 21a) relates that he beseeched the A-mighty for his condition as punishment for not rushing to help a poor, starving man fast enough. He went to get food, but felt that he was too slow and the man died. Knowing that his condition was exactly what he needed enabled him to accept it with incredible strength of character.

This awareness gave Rabbi Akiva the courage to begin studying Torah at the age of 40 and to continue even though initially he found it difficult. Whenever minor or major setbacks occurred, Rabbi Akiva immediately understood that they were totally for his benefit. When Rabbi Akiva's multitude of students died in a plague, he had the courage to begin again. And when Rabbi Akiva was tortured to death by the Romans, he courageously expressed his love for the Creator by serenely repeating *Shema Yisrael*.

As you develop the awareness that all is for the good in your own life, you will find yourself developing courage in ways that you might not have previously imagined.

# 8.

# WHAT IS THE HEROIC CHOICE?

When you consistently make heroic choices, you create a heroic life. You are constantly writing your autobiography, even if it is not written on paper. The choices you make are the material which shape your autobiography. When you make heroic choices, you create a heroic masterpiece.

There are many forms of heroic masterpieces. Some have become famous legends for their heroism. Ultimately everyone, including you, can live a life that is a heroic masterpiece.

Each heroic masterpiece is different from any other. Overcoming difficulties, suffering, handicaps, obstacles, and limitations are part of the drama of such a masterpiece. Everyone has his or her fair share of these.

At each point of choice and decision, one would be wise to ask oneself, "What would be the choice to take to create my unique heroic masterpiece?" At times this is a decision that means continuing on the same path. At times this is a decision to move somewhere else. At times it is clear which choice actually is heroic. And at times it is not. At times it is the choice to speak up, and at other times it is the choice to remain silent, or to listen. At times, it is the choice to take some action, and at other times it is the choice to refrain from taking action. At times it is a choice that requires a lot of thought, and at other times, thought is not needed, only action. At times you will feel good after you make this choice. At other times you will not, but it is still the choice to make.

The heroic choice might not always be recognized by anyone else as being the heroic choice. But when you know that what you are choosing is the heroic choice, it is an integral part of your heroic autobiography. May your heroic choices elevate you throughout your life.

*Looking back on many of the choices I made in life, I can see that I frequently made choices that were based on fear and intimidation. I didn't put it in these words while I was making those choices, but lack of courage was often a primary factor for my decisions. This affected my choice of friends, my choice of schools, my choice of jobs, and any other major decision that I needed to make.*

*But in my mid-40's, I made a heroic decision that changed me forever. A close relative of mine needed a kidney. I was asked whether I would be willing to be a donor. I was about to give a number of excuses why I wouldn't be able to do this. But I realized that my excuses were just rationalizations based on fear.*

*"This time you will make a choice out of courage,"* I emphatically told myself.

*My agreeing to undergo the surgery to save someone's life was the heroic choice that made the last fifteen years totally different from the previous years. This decision gave me a self-image of being a person with tremendous courage. Many choices I have made since then were choices that I would never have been able to make without that heroic decision.*

# 9.

# "THIS, TOO, WILL UPGRADE MY COURAGE"

**E**very time you upgrade your brain with courage in any context, you can create an automatic upgrade of courage in all contexts. This general principle is true for all attributes and states. It is especially important to realize this when it comes to courage.

There is a powerful slogan that will help us remember this valuable principle: "This, too, will upgrade my courage."

The more courage something takes, the more courage you have available for you for the rest of your life.

What this means for you is that if you are able to speak with courage in any context of your life, you can call upon that same inner resource to speak with courage in every other context. For example, some people are assertive with only certain types of people. With other people they feel limited. Realizing that there is a context where they have the courage to be assertive will enable them to be assertive in all situations.

There will be instances when you do something exceptionally courageous. Do not think, "I had courage here, but this really wasn't me. Normally I can't do these type of things." It is much wiser to think, "This has upgraded the courage level of my brain." You are no longer on the previous level of courage, but on the present level. This is your actual reality.

What if you are working on upgrading courage and you react in a way that is the opposite of courage? Does this mean that you are always going to lack that courage? Of course not! If someone were working on increasing their level of fear or cowardice, then they could gleefully say, "This is great. Now I have increased my fear level." Or they could say, "This is fantastic. Now I have a free upgrade of cowardice." But since you are working on increasing courage, every courageous word and deed is added to your brain's file labeled "courage." Don't empower the fear files in your brain. Those lapses serve as reminders that you will gain by increasing your level of courage. Every once in a while you might forget to call upon your courage. But it is always there. Keep exercising it and besides it becoming stronger, your recent use of courage increases your awareness that it is right there in your brain along with all of your other positive resources.

You do not have to wait until you do more courageous acts in the future. You can take anything that you ever said or did in the past that was an expression of courage and you can say now, "This, too, will upgrade my courage." You can even create a new mental picture of doing something courageous, and utilize this as part of your upgrading process.

*I tended to nod my head even if I didn't understand what was being said. I was embarrassed to ask for the definitions of words I didn't understand. I would always try to figure out what something meant from hearing the entire context. If someone was speaking too fast for me to follow what was said, I wouldn't feel comfortable to ask him to please speak more slowly. If it was noisy and I couldn't hear someone well, I found it difficult to ask him to repeat what he said, especially after the second or third time.*

*Then I started working on increasing my level of courage. I viewed each time I asked someone to define a term as an exercise in courage. And the same with asking people to speak more slowly as they explained things to me. "This, too, will upgrade my courage," I would say. Viewing speaking up as an act of courage, instead of feeling incompetent and insecure, I felt myself becoming increasingly strong.*

*It is often difficult for me to speak up. If I buy a food product that is spoiled, I prefer to throw it out, rather than return to the store to get a refund. Today, I bought eight yogurts. When waiting in line, I recalled the last time I had been in this store. I had told the man at the register that I had six yogurts, but when I arrived home I saw that I had taken only four. In the past, I might have just paid for the entire eight. But I was working on courage, so I told the owner that last time I had paid for two more than I took. He then charged me for only six yogurts. For me, speaking up was yet another step in increasing courage. I said to myself, "This, too, will upgrade my courage." I now feel that this type of action will be much easier for me.*

*I met someone who was in a concentration camp during World War II. He related a number of incidents he experienced, and how each day it took courage to just stay alive. He told me of the fear and terror that he had to overcome. He described how each minor act of secret defiance put one's life in danger. Thinking about this later, I said to myself, "There is a reason that I needed to hear this. This, took, will upgrade my courage."*

# 10.

# AN ACT OF COURAGE EACH DAY

E ach and every day look for an opportunity to do an act of courage. Some days this will be easy, too easy. You might find that the acts of courage that come your way are more than you bargained for. Other days, you might have to search for something you can say or do that will be an act of courage. The fact that you are seeking courage opportunities automatically makes you a more courageous person.

Any time you need to overcome resistance to do a positive action, you are doing an act of courage. Any time you ask a question that you find difficult to ask, you are doing an act of courage. Any time you request someone to do something for you and you find it difficult to make the request, you are doing an act of courage. Any time you find it difficult to correct someone, you are doing an act of courage.

At the onset of working on courage, you may decide that you want to do two or three acts of courage a day. Whatever number you accept upon yourself, if you do not reach your quota, it is worthwhile to add this to the next day's quota. By doing this, you are likely to find extra acts of courage that you can do.

When you actively seek acts of courage, you will feel much more positive about them when opportunities arise. Instead of viewing a difficult challenge as, "Oh no. I wish I wasn't in this situation." You will be able to say to yourself, "This is great. I will now be able to fill my quota for today."

*I feel that it's very important to guard one's health. In the past, I have observed people doing things that are unhealthy for them, but I felt uncomfortable about making positive suggestions. Now that I made a commitment to do three courageous acts a day, I look around for opportunities to make gentle suggestions. I make every effort that even if someone isn't open to actually follow what I tell him, he will appreciate my sincere concern.*

*It is a very high priority for me to use outcome wording when giving feedback or making suggestions to people. Outcome wording is when you make your request not as an attack on what someone is doing wrong, but on what he can do correctly. This one factor makes a major difference in the way people speak to each other.*

*A non-outcome wording would be, "Don't talk like that. When you talk like that you will be hurting people's feelings. You will make enemies and you won't be successful in influencing people. No one likes to be spoken to in a negative way. Don't follow what I say and you will ruin your life."*

*Now compare that with outcome wording, "When you speak with the positive outcome in mind, you will motivate people better. People will see clearly that you are trying to help them and they are likely to appreciate your suggestions. You will enhance friendships and will have a greater influence on more lives. Follow what I'm suggesting and you will benefit greatly."*

*Parents who speak to their children in non-outcome ways will be causing problems. Married couples who speak to each other in a non-outcome manner will become embroiled in many quarrels. Teachers and employers will be causing pain and resentment. Conversely, outcome wording enhances relationships and creates harmony between people.*

*I am totally committed to suggest to those who speak in negative ways to speak pleasantly and respectfully with the outcome in mind. Sometimes I find this easy. But when I find it difficult, I use it as my own courage-building tool.*

# 11.

# COURAGE AND SELF-RESPECT

Courage builds self-respect. When you sacrifice for principles and ideals, you increase your self-respect. When you face a painful situation and react with dignity, you increase your self-respect. When you say, "No," to temptation even though others will try to persuade you to say, "Yes," you increase your self-respect. When you do not allow opposition to stop you from doing what you know must be done, you increase your self-respect. In short, every act of courage makes you feel better about yourself.

The converse is also true. Acting with cowardice decreases your self-respect. Allowing fear to prevent you from doing what needs to be done decreases your self-respect. If you ever find your self-respect decreased because of what you said or did or what you failed to say or do, do not simply stop there. Rather, build your self-respect by doing what is difficult for you to do.

You might surprise yourself. You might view yourself as having a limited amount of courage. But then you face a major danger and you do something that takes much more courage than you ever thought you had. Your entire view of yourself can take a major leap forward. By mentally preparing yourself in advance for such a moment, you will be much more likely to rise to the challenge. Just thinking about this possibility will immediately have a positive effect on how you view yourself.

*My entire body language used to make a statement that I lacked self-esteem. When I spoke, it was clear that I didn't feel positive about myself. A teacher of mine asked me what prevents me from having more self-respect.*

*"I'm a coward," I replied with embarrassment. "How can I feel positively about myself when I'm so afraid of so many things?"*

*"Regardless of how many fears you have and how much they limit you, your value is intrinsic. You are created in the image of the Creator. You are a beloved child of the Creator. And you are obligated to say, 'The universe was created for me.' When you internalize these basic Torah concepts, you will inevitably have self-respect," my teacher said.*

*"In theory you are right," I acknowledged. "But in practice, my fears stop me from feeling self-respect."*

*"What do you feel you need to do to have more self-respect?" I was asked.*

*"I don't know what I can do. My intellect is average. I don't see myself as being a great scholar. I'm what one would call mediocre," I replied.*

*"Over the next few days make a list of things that you refrain from*

saying or doing out of fear," my teacher said.

"That will be easy for me," I replied.

And it was easy. In just a few days I had a list of twenty-five items. I could have added to this list, but I felt that this was sufficient for now. When I reported to my teacher, I jokingly said, "At least this is one that I did successfully."

My teacher looked carefully at the list and then said to me, "That was the easy part. Now for the hard part. What I am going to tell you to do might at first seem impossible. But I will be your coach and I'm positive that you will be successful. The list of wenty-five things is a list of your new goals. I will keep encouraging you and will give you some tools that will help you do them. Remember how you used to feel about yourself before you started doing those things. I assure you that you will feel like a different person after you take action on what you feared to do.

"The beginning will be difficult," he added, "but it will become easier and easier as you have fewer items on your list."

That's exactly what happened. After doing a few of those things, I did feel better about myself. Since I saw that I was able to do what I didn't think I could, it gave me the belief that it was just a matter of time until I would be able to do most of the things on that list.

I remember clearly the day that I was able to check off all twenty-five items. My self-image had improved drastically. Not only did I feel this on the inside. Other people I knew kept remarking to me that I seem so much more confident than I ever did before. My body language and tone of voice mirrored my new self-respect.

# 12

# EARNING THE RESPECT OF OTHERS

P eople respect courage. When someone acts with true courage, he is respected. This is most strongly experienced when a person risks his own life or serious injury in order to save someone else's life. This is experienced when someone has the courage of his convictions and willingly makes major sacrifices. At times people detect a quiet sense of courage in a certain person and over time realize that this is a person with courage. That individual is invariably respected.

All this would not apply if people feel that someone is only acting in ways that seem courageous but is motivated out of a desire for glory or to gain the approval of others. Genuine courage is valuable, while fake courage is like a fake diamond. It might appear at first like the real thing. But it is in an entirely different category. It might look expensive, but it is just a cheap piece of glass.

What is the difference between the first category and the second? Genuine courage is when the person taking action is motivated by ideals, principles, and the goodness of one's heart. The respect of others is a byproduct. Such a person would act with courage even if no one else would ever know about his courageous actions. Moreover, with true courage even the disapproval of others would not stop that person from taking action. That is exactly what makes this person courageous.

If a person only acts with courage because he wants glory or approval, it is not the essence of courage that is motivating him. Rather, he wants honor and respect, and the courageous action is just a means to an end. If he thinks that no one will know about his bravery, he will either make certain that they do or he will not take action. If such a person knows that he might meet with disapproval, he will not take action or speak up unless he knows that more people will approve than disapprove. This is not always measured in numbers, but in the subjective significance of the person or persons whose approval he thinks he will gain.

Courage for honor might at times be an important step in the right direction. The Sages tell us to be involved in Torah study and doing good deeds even if our motivations are not elevated. Our involvement in these actions will lead to higher motivations. A person who acts with courage to gain respect is still doing something that takes courage. Therefore it is a step up the ladder and might eventually lead to pure motivations.

*During the Second World War, a Nazi officer came over to my mother and said that he was going to shoot her. "Turn around and look away!" he cruelly shouted at her.*

*"If you are going to shoot me, you will have to look me straight in the eyes," she bravely replied. The Nazi shrugged his shoulders and didn't shoot.*

*Another woman who witnessed this mistakenly thought that here was a compassionate Nazi and pleaded with him to save her life. The Nazi immediately shot and killed her. (Heard from Rabbi Menashe Feiger about his mother)*

# 13.

# MELTING UNDER ANALYSIS

There are many illusory fears that will melt under analysis. When you find something difficult for you to do, ask yourself, "What exactly am I afraid of?" Often you will find that your fears have no basis in reality. In other instances, there might be a slight loss, but it is actually quite minor and trivial.

A similar question is, "What is the worst that could happen if I say or do this?" Often, your answer will be, "Nothing much."

Another question is, "How probable is it that I will actually suffer if I say or do this?" When you ask someone for some information or even to buy something or donate money, the worst that will happen is that he will refuse to give you the information, he will refuse to buy what you are selling, or he will refuse to give a donation. If you had not asked, you surely would not get the information, the sale, or the donation. So when you ask, the worst-case scenario is exactly the same as if you had not asked. Asking has the potential for improving the situation and you have nothing to lose.

*If I am looking for a certain building, I often find it difficult to ask people for directions. But when I asked myself, "What exactly am I afraid of?" I saw that there was actually nothing at all. The vast majority of people I have asked for directions in my life have either given me the directions I needed, or told me that they don't know. At times, someone might give me the wrong directions, but since without asking the person I didn't know where to go, I had to take that risk. Once in a long while someone will just walk by without answering me, but that is rare.*

*I was on an airplane for an overseas flight. I saw a father leave an infant on the seat and then walk away for a few minutes. I was seated a few rows behind him across the aisle. I thought to myself, "I should really go over and stand near that baby and then tell the father to be more careful." But I felt uncomfortable about doing this. I do have a tendency to be more nervous about these type of things than most people. And maybe this was another instance when I was overly concerned. If I would have had more courage to get involved with these strangers, I would have walked over. I figured that since the airplane had still not taken off, the baby probably wouldn't fall. But I felt nervous while I watched. Then the father returned and I felt a sense of relief that the situation was safe.*

*I was reading a book and didn't pay attention to them anymore. A few minutes later, I heard the noise of something falling. It was that infant. The father immediately ran back to his seat and you could tell that he loved his child. The mother, who was seated several rows away, was very aggravated. Fortunately the infant wasn't injured. But now I am totally dedicated to approach anyone who would do anything similar and tell them that they need to be more careful. What is the worst thing that could happen if I tell a parent or baby-sitter to be more careful? Someone might become irritated that I am interfering. But it's clear that it's preferable for them to be irritated with my suggestion than for an infant to be harmed.*

*I find it difficult to praise people or to give positive feedback. I did not grow up with this. I considered my praising anyone as not being authentically myself. When I gave the matter deeper thought, I realized that I was afraid that people would consider me insincere if I praised them. Was I really sincere? Yes. Therefore anyone who would consider me insincere would be making an error. It was suggested that I work on courage. As long as I am really sincere, I should begin to praise those who would appreciate it. The first few times I tried, I found it difficult. I now find it easy to praise people, even those I don't know well. What negative experiences have I had with this? None!*

# 14.

# LEARN FROM THE COURAGE OF OTHERS

E very act of courage of others that you personally observe is now part of your own mental database of courage. You have a model you can learn from. The same applies to every act of courage of others that you hear or read about.

Some people hear or read about the courage of others and view it as that person's behavior. They tell themselves, "I could never do that." But you can. First of all there might always be circumstances that would enable you to say and do things that you thought you would never be able to say or do. A mother who sees that her child is in danger might have incredible strength and courage that she would have never dreamed of. A man might think that he would never be able to be a successful salesman. He feels that he is too shy or introverted. Then he finds a selling job with an unbelievably high commission. For the amount of money he would now earn, he would be able to try to sell to the most difficult customer. A person might feel that he would never be able to speak in public the way a specific dynamic speaker does. Then he takes a public-speaking course. There he is taught to model great speakers. An issue comes up that he cares deeply about and he surprises himself with how well he speaks.

The starting point is to be aware that if someone else can do something and you do the exact same thing that he does, you will get the same results. Of course, there is innate talent. If someone is lacking these, he is not likely to do as well as a person who is naturally gifted. But when it comes to speaking and acting with courage, it is a pattern that you can emulate and model. You can rerun the scenes in your mind over and over again until you know that you will actually be able to act that way when opportunities arise.

You do not have to wait until you witness new scenes of courage to act with courage. If you have lived on our planet long enough to learn how to read this book, it is inevitable that you have seen, heard, and read about many acts of courage. You have seen people who have spoken up for their rights. You have heard public speakers. You have seen and heard people influencing others to do or buy things. You have read about people who did what was difficult to do because of their ideals and principles. Even if those ideals and principles are different from yours, the pattern from which you can benefit is still there for you.

From this moment on, every new act of courage you see or hear and read about can be viewed as part of your lifetime program of learning how to speak and act with courage. You will be more aware of this attribute wherever you are and wherever you go. You will observe what you would have missed out on had you not been viewing the courage of others as yours to model and learn from.

*I have a friend who raises funds for distribution to families in financial need. He spends much time and energy on this project. "Do you find it difficult to ask people for money?" I asked him.*

*"I'm not doing this for myself so why should I find this difficult?" was his response. Because he had altruistic motivations, he found this easy to do. Regardless of whether someone would or would not contribute, he knew that he was doing the right thing by asking them. Before speaking to him, I found doing something similar extremely difficult. Shortly after hearing this from him, I had an opportunity to raise funds for someone who was in dire financial need. With my friend as a role model, it was relatively easy for me.*

*I once met a taxicab driver who told me that he has a life mission to stop people from smoking cigarettes. When they are in his taxicab, he has a captive audience. This is something that I have felt for a long time that I should also do. But I've found it difficult. "If this person can do it, so can I," I said to myself. Ever since then, I have been more outspoken and tell people that they would be wise to stop.*

*I once heard a radio interview with one of the most outspoken obnoxious people I have ever heard. The person's positions on impor-*

*tant issues were not based on facts and data, but on mistaken assumptions and prejudice. I felt my blood boiling. I was furious that someone could publicly take a stand that was so preposterous.*

*Then I remembered to look for what I could learn from this person. I recalled what I read from Rabbi Elchonon Wasserman on the statement of the Sages about King Solomon. The verse states that he was the wisest of people. The Midrash adds, "Even from people who were crazy." This can be understood in various ways. Rav Elchonon understood that this means King Solomon was able to gain wisdom from everyone, even from someone who is irrational and not living in reality.*

*So I said to myself, "The same way that this person speaks up and doesn't worry if anyone else will agree with his position, I can also speak up. I feel that what I have to say needs to be heard." The first few times I had to force myself. Then it became easier. If I ever find the fear coming back, I just recall this individual and other people like him and once again I am able to spread the important ideas that I feel people should be aware of.*

*Growing up I viewed myself as lacking courage. When I heard that you can take on the attitudes, beliefs, and ways of being of any other person by just pretending for a while that you are that person, I decided that I would pretend I was a mixture of the most courageous people I have ever met and the most courageous people I have ever read about and the most courageous people I could ever imagine. I realized that this was extreme, but if you would know how far I really was from this, you would understand why I needed such drastic measures.*

*I still lived in reality. But I was dedicated to follow the concept that the past does not equal the future. The amount of courage that I will have now is not based on the courage I had before, but on the courage that I decide I have at this very moment. And I decided that I was going to live with the awareness that the Creator can bestow courage on anyone, even me.*

*I was careful not to think or act like anyone who was arrogant or conceited. Rather, I would pretend to be supercourageous, while at the same time be totally careful to think about the outcomes and consequences of anything I would say and do. I wasn't going to prove to anyone else that I was courageous. I was just going to experience it myself, especially in the areas in which I was previously limited.*

*The results were simply amazing. I immediately began feeling more powerful and courageous that I ever felt before. I felt empowered as I walked down the street, when I walked into a room of strangers, and when I spoke on the telephone.*

*After pretending to be courageous for an entire month, I no longer needed to pretend. What I previously had viewed as the states of others now became my very own reality.*

# 15

# INTERVIEW PEOPLE WITH COURAGE

veryone can be an interviewer. All you need to do is ask questions. Whenever you meet someone who has exceptional courage or has evidenced courage in those areas that you still do not, ask him how he creates it.

Some people you view as having courage might not see themselves in that light. They just say and do things that they find easy. Ask them what they tell themselves, what they visualize, and how they feel when they do the specific things that are difficult for you.

When you ask these questions some people are able to answer clearly. Others might begin by telling you that they do not know. They just do it. Be patient and ask them to think of something they find too difficult to do or say. When they think of a specific situation, ask them to describe the differences in what they tell themselves, what they picture, and how they feel.

People who at one time could not do something and now can are often the best people to interview. Since they had to work on courage, they will often be able to give you a clearer picture of the changes they made. They might be able to describe the distinctions in thoughts, imagery, and feelings between when they were not able to act with courage and when they were.

*Whenever I meet someone who has undertaken an adventure, I ask him questions to find out how he handled what he did. My experience has been that you will always meet the type of people you are seeking. Just this week, I met someone who together with a partner crossed the Atlantic Ocean in a small boat. The most memorable part of the trip occurred when they bumped into a whale. Another fellow described how eighteen years before he was arrested by security officers when he was taking a tour of the White House in Washington. It seems that he had an uncanny resemblance to someone they were looking for who had sent a threatening letter. Only after a number of hours of intense interrogation did they realize that he was not that person. I spoke to a prosecutor who had confronted some very tough adversaries. And I met someone who was badly injured in a terrorist attack and made a remarkable recovery as a result of tremendous inner strength. Asking questions about how each one handled the difficulties they experienced gave me more insight into courage. You, too, will be able to gain from the courage experiences of others by using the power of questions.*

*I always wanted to interview people to learn from their experiences. But something held me back. I was afraid that people would consider my questions to be intrusive and bothersome.*

*I asked my friend who found it easy to interview people how he did it. "Don't they become annoyed?" I asked him.*

*"You're doing an interview right now," he replied. "I'm happy that I can help you. Asking others is just like asking me. And you see that you can do this."*

*"Yes, but you're a friend of mine," I said.*

*"That's it," he said. "View every person you encounter as a close friend. Some won't like your asking them questions. Be aware of their tone of voice and facial expression. When you are sincerely interested in how a person does something and want to learn from him, he will gladly tell you how he does it. Observe to see if someone seems uncomfortable. Apologize and interview someone else."*

*I asked others these type of questions and I found that my friend was right. Most people I asked were happy to share their knowledge. They felt good about helping another person.*

# 16.
# GO TO THE OPPOSITE EXTREME

When discussing character development, Maimonides (*Hilchos Dei'os* 1:2) states that the goal is the middle path in each trait. But in order to get there, we need to behave with the opposite extreme for a time. Once we are accustomed to the extreme, we can then revert to the middle.

Think of courageous actions you can take that previously would have been too difficult for you. We are not referring to doing things that might cause injury. If you ever find yourself in real need to do something dangerous, the need of the moment will increase your level of courage to do it. To mentally prepare yourself for these moments, visualizations are a lot safer and you do not need to actually risk injury to yourself. But there are many emotional risks that would be considered going to the opposite extreme.

There were educators who had their students engage in special exercises to overcome fear of what other people might think. The most famous were the ones used in Novaradok.

There they were told to ask for bread in a hardware store and for hammers in a bakery. This method is not feasible for everyone. But we can all do things that are more usual but that are difficult for us.

Look for opportunities to make public announcements that you would ordinarily consider difficult to make.

Greet people you have never greeted before.

If you are afraid to ask people for directions, go out of your way to ask for directions wherever you are until you find it easy to do.

If you are afraid to ask questions of teachers, ask at least three questions each class (as long as the teacher is comfortable with this).

If you never asked anyone to donate money to charity, keep asking until you find it easy.

If you feel uncomfortable talking to strangers, speak to strangers when waiting in lines, when attending weddings and other joyous occasions, when traveling on public transportation, and every opportunity you get.

If you are afraid to speak in public, go out of your way to volunteer to speak as often as you can until you find it easy to do.

*I was visiting relatives in a city that was far from where I lived. The newspaper had the story of someone who had donated $50 million to an educational institution. I felt that here was a great opportunity to build up my courage. I wasn't fund-raising and I wasn't* *planning to ask this person for money. But I wanted to prove to myself that I could make a cold call to this man's office and ask for a short interview. Talking to the donor of such a large amount was a way of building up my belief in what was possible for me. I felt a bit of trepidation when dialing the telephone. But I got the interview. Ever since that moment I knew that the sky was the limit with regard to whom I could contact.*

# 17.

# VISUALIZING COURAGE

V isualize courage. Your magnificent brain can draw mental pictures of how you would like to speak and act. The more times you replay these pictures, the easier it will be for you to follow through in reality. Utilize this gift from the Creator to increase your level of courage.

Think of ways that you would like to speak and act that you presently find difficult to do. Make mental pictures of yourself speaking and acting with joyous empowerment. Do not be concerned whether your mental pictures are clear or dim. Even if you don't actually see a clear picture, this powerful tool will work for you.

You may wish to start with something that is only slightly difficult for you. Then when you visualize this enough times, you will be able to upgrade the difficulty of the situations. After a while, you will be able to visualize situations that previously seemed impossible for you.

You may prefer to begin with the most difficult situations.

After visualizing the seemingly impossible, less stressful situations will be relatively easier.

Visualize yourself maintaining both self-respect and respect for the person with whom you are speaking. Know your goal. Say what would be helpful to achieve that goal in a way that is sensitive to the individuality of the recipient of your message. For example, if you feel that someone is trying to overcharge you, do not visualize yourself screaming and berating that person. Rather, see yourself saying, "I'm sure you agree that it's important to be fair. Let's make our transaction in a way that is fair to both of us."

Visualize yourself following through on specific actions that manifest courage. In the mental theater of your brain, picture yourself being able to do the most courageous things that a human being could possibly do.

In the Talmud we find that the great sage Rabbi Akiva was tortured by the cruel Romans. As he neared death Rabbi Akiva serenely recited *Shema Yisrael*; he proclaimed the Oneness of the Creator during his final moments in this world. His students who were in captivity nearby called out to him, "Our teacher, how can you remain serene at this moment?"

"I have waited for this moment my entire life," replied Rabbi Akiva.

Every time Rabbi Akiva recited *Shema Yisrael*, he mentally visualized himself giving up his life because of his love of G–d. After years of this daily mental training, he had perfected it to such a degree that even his students, who had come to know Rabbi Akiva's greatness, were astounded by his serenity. The altered state that he mastered enabled him to transcend all physical pain. Please note that Rabbi Akiva said he had waited for this moment his entire life. It took him his entire life to reach this level, and Rabbi Akiva lived to the age of 120. As we strive to reach lofty levels we need to practice consistently. The striving itself is an act of greatness and each time we practice we are elevating ourselves spiritually.

*I used to be terrified of taking tests. The anxiety I experienced greatly diminished my ability to think clearly. The grades that I would receive on tests were way below my actual knowledge. I had a principal who was very sensitive to this issue. He told me he realized that I'm bright and that when I am calm, I have easy access to the knowledge in my brain. He gave me two tools. First, I should breathe slowly and deeply and keep repeating to myself, "Calm and relaxed." After a few minutes of this, a lot of my tension and stress would be released. Secondly, he told me to practice visualizing myself being totally cool, calm, and collected when I took tests. I could practice any time I had a few minutes to myself. He reassured me that eventually, I would even enjoy taking tests. This was something that I couldn't believe would ever happen. But it did. The first time I felt calm while taking a test was to me a real miracle. I now feel positive about the tests I take. I need to add that he also told me that during the tests I should visualize myself reading the textbook we had studied and to mentally picture* my notes. I could also visualize myself sitting in class listening to the teacher. I have used this method for other fears and the results have been amazing.

A friend of mine went to a workshop where the speaker shared with the audience that when he was young he had a list of fears that was awesome. He was afraid of dogs and cats. He was afraid of the dark. He was afraid of the water. He was afraid of bugs, insects, and snakes. He was afraid of asking anyone for anything and was afraid to speak in public. He was afraid of lightning and thunder. He was afraid of airplanes and of heights. If there was a fear to have, he had it.

What did he do to overcome his many fears? He used visualizations. He imagined being in a cage with lions. In such a situation, fear of the lions would arouse their anger and viciousness. Only by remaining totally calm and serene could one handle the lions in a way that they would remain placid. He visualized being calm and serene the entire time he was in the same cage with the lions. He mentally repeated this over and over again. He did this so frequently that it helped him overcome all his fears. Eventually he was in a situation where he was in a cage by himself with a wild jaguar. When he had mentally practiced similar scenarios he never really thought that this would one day be a skill that he would utilize to save his life. His mental training had conditioned him with the ability to remain calm. He safely moved around the cage until he could open the door and exit unharmed.

I have found that visualizing myself being able to do this has helped me cope with many difficult situations that I previously feared.

# 18

# COURAGE IS A STATE

ourage is a state. You do not have to be a person who feels courageous all the time in order to speak and act with courage. You can be in a joyous state for a few minutes, even if you are not always joyous. You can be in a serene state for a while, even if you are not always serene. You can be in a centered and balanced state, even if you are not always this way. The same applies to courage.

When you are fearful, do not define yourself as a fearful person. Rather, view the situation as, "Right now I am in a fearful state." Similarly, if you feel too fearful to ask a question or to express your disagreement, do not view this as your entire way of being. Rather, view it as a state you are presently in. Even though you are in a nonresourceful state right now, you have the ability to access a more resourceful state.

Did you ever change a state in a moment? Of course you did. We all do a multitude of times. Someone might be feeling a bit sad, and then he hears something hilariously funny. In just one second, he may go from being in a down state to a humorous state. Someone might be in a bored state. Then he hears someone talking about a way he can earn a large amount of money. He immediately goes into an excited state. Someone may be angry with a specific person, even furious. Then he hears an air-raid siren and the anger is forgotten. When a few minutes later he finds out that this was not a nuclear attack, but a false alarm, his state will change to one of relief.

We all have the ability to access a state of courage. At times we might find this easy and at times it could be difficult. The more times you practice accessing courage, the easier it will become even in situations where you previously were not able to do so.

How do you access a state? In my book *Begin Again Now*, I have a list. Here are some of the ways to apply this to courage.

• Change your body language and your way of speaking to that of courage. Sit, stand, or walk the way you do when you feel courageous or confident. Talk with the tone of voice you use when you feel courageous. Breathe the way you breathe when you experience courage. Let your facial expression be the same as it is when you feel courageous. Do not just read this. Test it out. Be congruent. As you do this, realize that it will work when you do it right.

I have seen some people access a state of joy while saying, "I can't just stand and smile with joy and then feel joyous." Since they were expressing their belief that they could not do this, they did not resist. Then they were naturally able to access the resourceful state they claimed they could not do. People who do this often need someone else to give them feedback that they have actually accessed the positive state. The same applies to courage.

- Remember a time in the past when you felt courageous. Picture the scene vividly. Mentally make it large and close and colorful. Talk and act in ways that are similar to how you spoke and acted then. Feel what you felt then. In the present you can even intensify the positive feelings and make them stronger than they were originally.

- Imagine what it would be like if you had courage in the future. Imagine that you have been given the ultimate in courage as a gift from the Creator. This would be so much a part of you that it would feel natural and you would take it for granted as the way you are. Picture how you would speak and act. View other people and the entire world from the perspective of courage. Hear the way you would sound when you speak with others and when you talk to yourself. Allow yourself to feel these feelings right now. Since you are projecting to a time in the future it is easier not to block yourself. When you create a feeling of courage, you can then utilize it now.

- Imagine being someone who is the epitome of courage with modesty. Hear and see yourself speaking like that person speaks. Visualize yourself acting the way that person acts. Imagine that you have this person's energy and experience the feelings of courage that you now can utilize for the good.

• Create an anchor. That is, when you feel an intense feeling of courage, make a hand movement or a sound, or both, that your mind can now associate with courage. Intensify your courage, and repeat the hand movement or the sound. You might clasp your hands together and say the word "courage." Or you might move a finger the way you would when pressing a key on a computer. See the word "courage" on your mental computer screen and feel courage spreading from head to toe. Some people find it easy to create this on their own. Others could use a coach to help them with the process.

• Repeat the word "courage" over and over again calmly and slowly as you breathe slowly and deeply. With each repetition feel yourself becoming more courageous.

# 19.
# A COURAGE PART

I f you are not yet able to access a powerful courage state at will, the good news is that you can create a courage part. Even if you do not feel that you are a courageous person, you can still have a part that can speak and act from a place of courage.

There are people who say, "Part of me wants to do this or that and part of me doesn't feel like doing it." Or, "I have a part of me that stops me from doing such and such." These people feel as if they had different parts. This can be utilized positively. Whenever you need any state or way of being, you can view yourself as having the appropriate part.

Most likely you already have a courageous part. This is the part of you that has already spoken or acted with courage in specific situations. In the future, if you need a burst of courage, have your courage part take over.

Let your courage part say what you yourself find hard to say. Let your courage part make that difficult telephone call. Let your courage part take over in a situation where you feel overly self-conscious. Let your courage part negotiate for you if you begin to feel intimidated.

If you do not yet have a courage part, create one. Do a single act of courage, even a minor one. If this does not come easily, use the entire force of your will to say or do something that is difficult for you. Then presto! Your courage part is now a reality. If you cannot yet do this in reality, create your courage part by utilizing your power of imagination. Imagine yourself talking and acting with courage. Then your courage part can apply this in real life. If it is that easy, why is it that everyone does not do this? O.K., so it is not that easy. But it does work and in a very powerful way. And when you do this, you might find it easier than you thought.

Every time you exercise your courage part, it becomes stronger. When you exercise it enough, it will be integrated into your own self. You will eventually consider yourself courageous and will spontaneously be able to do the things for which you needed your courage part.

*I hoped to be accepted to a school which I felt was perfect for my needs. I didn't do so well in the school I had attended. I was intensely determined to study better. I felt awful when I was told that due to my past record, they wouldn't accept me. In the past I would have given up right away. But I had heard about allowing my courage part to take over. I did. I acknowledged my past failures as a student.*

*"Now I am totally committed to use all of my potential that people used to tell me I had," I told the principal. "I will work so hard that you will consider accepting me one of the wisest decisions you ever made."*

*Normally, I couldn't speak like this. But it was my courage part speaking. And my courage part can say anything that is needed to be said. I was accepted and did well. My courage part has gotten much stronger since then from all the use I've given it.*

*I was on a city bus and noticed that the bus driver was very impatient. He would try to close the door before the passengers were off. He wouldn't wait for anyone who was running for the bus. He spoke rudely to the passengers. I felt that he needed to be spoken to. But I was too timid to speak up. However, my courage part was not too timid. It took over and with sensitivity and respect told the driver that it's important for him to learn to be more patient. I saw that he took what I said seriously. I don't know yet how much he will change, but at least I know I did what I could. As I walked back to my seat, someone in the front seat thanked me. He frequently was on the bus with this driver and most people didn't try to have a positive influence on him.*

*"If more people would speak to him as respectfully as you just did, I'm sure it will help," he said to me.*

*I don't feel comfortable negotiating for myself. I have observed people who love to negotiate. They easily say things that the other side won't like. They don't flinch when the other party says things that they don't like. I found myself in a situation where I had a strong need to negotiate. My initial reaction was, "I can't do this." But then I remembered that I have "an expert negotiator part." This part is totally, intensely courageous.*

*"Go for it!" I said to that part.*

*I kept the focus reaching a win-win outcome. I wanted to be fair to the other side. At the same time, I wanted to be fair to myself. This successful negotiation is now an integral part of me for the future.*

# 20.
# ACT "AS IF"

" What if I feel that I don't have any courage at all within me, not even a tiny courage part?"

There is a powerful tool that will help with courage and many other attributes: Act "as if" you had as much courage as you need. Do not do this to prove to anyone else that you have courage. Rather, do this in order to access a state of courage. As you speak and act "as if" you had courage, you will be integrating and internalizing this trait. Eventually you will have genuine attitudes and feelings of courage.

Experience is a great antidote to fear. If you are afraid to do something and you actually do it a number of times, it gets easier. When you do something by acting "as if" you had the courage to do it, the actual experiences automatically build up your knowledge that you can do the thing that you previously feared to do.

Take care not to sabotage your efforts. As you act "as if" you had courage, do not tell yourself, "What I'm doing is not really courage, since I am just acting 'as if.' " If you define your words and actions as "not really courage," you needlessly limit yourself. It takes courage to act "as if" you had courage. Since this is an actual manifestation of courage, you have a 100 percent right to consider your words "words of courage" and your actions "actions of courage."

*I needed a job. Even so I procrastinated and delayed going on job interviews. I found them too nerve wracking. I went for a few, but when I got turned down I needed a few days to recuperate and to build up my strength.*

*"Call on your inner courage," I was told.*

*"My inner courage is so weak that it can't speak above a whisper," I replied.*

*During this time, I read that if you act "as if" you were joyous, this increases your actual level of joy. This is even measurable on biofeedback machines and with the hormones in one's blood. "If this works for joy, perhaps it can work for courage," I said to myself.*

*The next day I was resolved to go for at least three interviews. Each time I walked through the door I would say to myself, "I am now going to act 'as if' I had tremendous courage. I will feel the way I would feel if I had total confidence. I will walk and talk the way I would if I were to have intense courage."*

*I still didn't feel as strong as someone who is naturally courageous. But this did give me a greater feeling of courage than I ever had before. I guess that this helped me make a better impression on the person doing the hiring, and the third interview was a success.*

*Since then I have used the power of "as if" many times. The way I am improving I feel certain that in the near future I won't need this tool. My courage will be spontaneous and automatic.*

*Reading about a professional stuntman changed my life. He was famous for engaging in the most dangerous stunts humanly possible.*

*"How are you able to not be afraid?" he was asked.*

*"I'm not able to," he smiled.*

*"But you look so confident when you perform your amazing stunts," he was challenged. "The vast majority of humanity are too frightened to do even less frightening things."*

*"I'm a normal human being," he replied. "Sure, I'm scared. But I behave as if I wasn't and take action."*

*I don't have to do anything resembling what he does. So I, too, began to act as if I had more courage and I now say and do positive things that I would never have believed I would be able to say and do. I consistently surprise myself.*

# 21

# THE INNER VOICE

Whenever you tell yourself that you cannot say or do something that is in your best interests to say or do, ask yourself, "What stops me?" This short three-word question is a great tool to stop yourself from being stopped by irrational fears.

One common pattern that tends to stop people is that they hear an inner voice telling them that they cannot do something. "What would happen if I did?" is the next question. At times there are valid reasons for not doing something that one has a right to do. When dealing with someone violent, it is often not in one's best interests to say all that is on one's mind. When talking to someone in authority, you would be wise not to talk back if that person is not open to hearing what you have to say and would consider anything you say insubordination and insolence.

The "What stops me?" question will often point out that nothing harmful or dangerous is stopping us. It is only an initial feeling of fear that gets in the way. This fear is sometimes in the form of an inner voice saying things like, "It's dangerous," without the danger being specified. And when you ask yourself, "What danger?" the answer is just a vague feeling of fear without any real danger.

Or an inner voice might say, "You never were able to do this before, so you cannot do it now." The question to ask yourself is, "Why not?" Often, the answer is, "Well, that's just the way it is." And this often means that it is a vague fear without a valid basis. When we were infants we were incapable of doing anything. That means that all the things you are able to say and do right now are things that at one time you could not do. When you think about this, it is amazing how this will open you up to continuously learning new things. Especially if there are things that at one time you thought you could not do and now you can, you will realize there will always be other positive things that you can still learn to say and do.

Sometimes one's inner self has a general feeling that something is not safe and cannot specify why. When this is a strong intuition even if one cannot explain it clearly, it could be that there is a subconscious valid reason for not saying or doing something. But when you feel that there really is not a valid reason and the fear is more in the category of a phobia, do not allow it to stop you. You have the ability to quiet the inner voice.

Thank the inner voice for trying to protect you. And then you can ask it to remain dormant until a real danger comes along. Learning to quiet one's inner voice in order to maintain a state of serenity is a valuable skill.

If an inner voice is just the voice of someone you knew who was excessively fearful, allow a more powerful inner voice of reason to resonate with messages such as, "What you are about to do is for your benefit. Go for it!"

When the thing that you would like to do is an elevated action and that the inner voice says to you, "Who are you to do such a good thing?" you can respond to it by saying, "I am a child of the Creator!"

# 22

# CHANGING THE PICTURE

Imaginary pictures can stop a person from doing things that are relatively safe to do. For example, some people panic when going on a bridge. When they become aware of the inner mental pictures, they will realize that they see a picture of the bridge collapsing. If the bridge is truly safe, then they need to create a picture of the bridge holding up under pressure.

Some people who are afraid of speaking in public have a mental picture of a time that they spoke and it turned out to be a total flop. Others create disaster pictures even if they were never the reality. If you do this, from now on remember a time you spoke well. Remember the scene in detail and keep this on the forefront of your mind. If this has not yet happened for you, you can still make a picture of this happening in the future. Some people visualize members of the audience staring at them with bulging eyes. They can now visualize members of the audience smiling friendly smiles. In reality, when you smile and nod to specific people in the audience, many will smile and nod back.

People who are claustrophobic and experience high levels of anxiety when they are in a small closed place often see the walls caving in. They can now make a picture of the walls being reinforced. They can also change the picture and visualize wide-open spaces.

People who are afraid to ask questions often visualize someone becoming angry at them for asking. This could be based on a past incident that happened to them or that they witnessed happening to someone else. It could even be a scene that never happened at all. To solve this they can create pictures of themselves asking questions and the people who are asked are grateful for the opportunity to do an act of kindness by answering the questions.

You have the ability to mentally melt the pictures that come to your mind. You might see them turning into ice and then the sun melts them. Or you might mentally create a special picture-melting machine.

You can also add humor to any scary pictures. You can think of funny scenes and then add lively music. You can visualize clowns jumping up and down or doing somersaults. You can mentally picture thousands of people laughing.

Some people find it very easy to do these visual exercises. Even people who do not visualize clearly have found it helpful to pretend to imagine these scenes.

## 23.

# TRANSFORM FEAR INTO COURAGE

From the perspective of courage, every time you experience fear you have another opportunity to increase your level of courage. With some situations, the very fact that your initial reaction is one of fear renders the words you say and the actions you take into courageous words and deeds. If you would be doing the very same thing and it would be easy for you, it would not be a courage-building event. Now that you were compelled to overcome your anxiety and fear, your level of courage is rising. This opens you up to a wealth of future possibilities that would not have been possible without the courage you are adding to your character.

If unwarranted fears prevent you from speaking up or taking action, view it as a reminder that you need to increase your level of courage. When you think about the situation, you can say to yourself, "I am totally motivated to transform this fear into courage." As you continue to build up this attribute, you will eventually be able to do the things that you now feared to do. When you are able to do those things in the future, that will serve as feedback that your courage is growing.

*I love the concept of transforming fear into courage. I wrote a note for myself, "Transform fear into courage," and I put this in a place where I would see it frequently. This has helped me immensely. It has served as a reminder to me that each and every day I will be able to increase my level of courage. I once attended a class where the speaker gave out sheets with an outline of his lecture before he began to speak. Somehow I and the two people sitting beside me didn't receive sheets. I didn't notice this at first because I was engaged in an absorbing conversation. A few minutes into the lecture, however, I realized that I hadn't received a copy of the outline. In the past, I would have just sat there without a sheet. But with my motto being, "Transform fear into courage," I stood up and brought back three sheets, one for myself and two for the people sitting next to me. For me this was a victory. I look forward to seeing all the minor and major things increased courage will enable me to do.*

*I found out that I needed to take a series of shots for a condition I had. I have memories of crying when I was given shots as a child. As an adult I didn't cry, of course. But I did feel greater anxiety then most adults. I would be very upset with myself for being such a baby. I had enough experience already to know that the pain of a shot is really minor. Now that my motto was "Transform fear into courage," I looked at the needles I had to endure as booster shots for more courage.*

I actually felt positive about these experiences. Wouldn't everyone be willing to take booster shots for courage? It gave me great pleasure to turn a potential liability into an asset.

I used to be obsessively afraid of cancer. Any time I heard that someone had cancer, I was shaken to the core. "That could be me," I said. Even hearing the word "cancer" in any context caused me much anxiety. A relative of mine died of cancer. For a long time prior to that, I was phobic about cancer and now that nervousness became stronger. It was suggested to me, "Transform fear into courage. The greater the fear, the greater the courage you will be attaining." Since my fear was intense, I needed super-intense courage to overcome that fear. From then on, every time I heard the word "cancer," I immediately heard an inner voice saying to me, "Transform fear into courage." Instead of living with constant stress about what might happen, I was now building up a general sense of empowerment. One major benefit was that I was able to help other people who had similar fears. I shared with those who would gain from it that I previously was obsessively anxious. And so my past obsession became a tool for kindness.

# 24.

# TRANSFORMING WORRY INTO A TOOL FOR COURAGE

Worry and courage have a lot in common. Both are emotional states. Both are created in one's mind. Both have an influence on what we will and will not do. As infants we are born with neither. Both will have a major impact on our character. And here they differ: Worry limits us and causes much distress. Courage expands our abilities and gives us feelings of hope and empowerment.

Worrying indicates the ability to project what might happen in the future. This shows that you can mentally create an emotional reaction based on what your brain focuses on. This same ability is how you can transform worry into a tool for courage.

Whenever you begin to worry, visualize yourself handling the situation, occurrence, or circumstance with courage. The more you used to worry, the more times you will be training your mind to react with courage. Your brain is active anyway. Make it work for you rather than against you.

Be patient when transforming worry into courage. Some people try two or three times and when they do not see immediate results, they become discouraged. They say to themselves, "This isn't going to work for me. My worry will stay. To worry is my nature and I'll always be this way." Since brains are open to programming and conditioning, this is exactly what one needs to tell oneself to sustain worry. The worrying thoughts appreciate this. They will be created and remembered. They will have a long and healthy life. But you who are the owner of your brain will have to pay a heavy price for this. It is not worth it.

When you are in the midst of a worry, ask yourself, "How would I like to handle this situation if it does happen?" Whatever you would like to say or do, you will do it best with courage. So you can now ask, "If I were to master the attribute of courage, what would I say or do to either improve the situation or to accept it with inner strength?" What was once a major liability will now be a major asset.

*I used to worry about my financial situation. "What will I do if I don't have the money I need?" was the question that I kept repeating to myself. This increased my anxiety and didn't allow me to think clearly about my options. When I changed my question to, "What will I be able to do when I increase my level of courage?" I felt intensely stronger. My mind was clearer and I felt much more optimistic about the future.*

*I was having difficulties getting married. I spent hours and hours worrying about how I would find the right person and what if I don't. When I was told to transform worry into courage, I immediately saw the benefits. Whenever I begin to get discouraged, I immediately hear an inner voice telling me, "Here is another reminder to increase my level of courage." I am much more optimistic now. And regardless of how the future unfolds, I know that now I will have more courage to deal with it.*

*As a parent I felt it was my duty to worry about my children. I would easily panic. I spoke with many other parents and it seemed that I worry more than the average. When I heard about the idea of transforming worry into courage, I began to change my thinking patterns. What encouraged me to do this is that I would be calmer when interacting with my children. And the emotional state of courage is the model that I want to transmit to my children.*

# 25.

# REWRITING PERSONAL HISTORY

Throughout our life we have behaved in ways that if we could do it over again, we would. The second time around, we would have learned from our mistakes of the first time. In actual reality, we are not able to replay the initial occurrence. But we do have a tool to change the effects of our past.

The name of this tool is "Rewriting personal history." In the Talmud (*Yoma* 86b) we find the concept that when we repent out of love for our Creator, the wrongs that we have done are now transformed into good deeds. That is because with our present awareness, we would have acted in a much more elevated way. As Rabbi Moshe Chaim Luzzatto writes in *Path of the Just*, this is a special kindness of our Loving Father, and powerful King. Here we see that there is a way that retroactively we can rewrite, as it were, our autobiography.

This tool is valuable when it comes to increasing courage. Our memories of lacking courage in the past can have a negative effect on our level of courage in the present. When we are in a situation similar to a time when we lacked courage before, we might lack courage in the present. But you can rerun those scenes. Since you are creating those mental pictures, you can visualize yourself handling situations the way you would have wanted to handle them the first time.

Try this with a specific single memory. Think of a time in the past that you lacked the necessary courage to handle a situation the way you would have preferred. Now rerun the scene in your mind the way you would have spoken and acted if you were to have a strong and powerful sense of courage. Feel the good feelings of knowing that from now on this memory will be a valuable resource for you.

Be patient when you do this. Those who visualize easily will find that they can do this without much effort. Others might find it difficult to change the way they view a past scene. But when they realize how powerful this tool is, they will be motivated to practice over and over again until they are able to do it.

All you need is one experience of changing the way the library in your brain stores a given memory to know that you will be able to do this with every memory. We mentioned with visualizations about the future that even if you do not see the picture clearly, it will still have an effect. The same applies to rewriting the scenes of the past. The very effort entailed to see yourself speaking and acting in courageous ways will be helpful.

Even if you do not go out of your way to edit and rewrite past scenes, if a fearful scene of the past comes up to your consciousness spontaneously, change the way you spoke and acted.

But isn't this falsifying the past? Not if you do it correctly. You know the reality of the way you actually acted. You want to change the effects of those words and actions. You want to use your present awareness to help you develop your character in the present regardless of what you did in the past.

*I tried rewriting my past memories of lack of courage, but I didn't feel I was getting anywhere with it. I consulted someone who had told me that this tool had worked for him.*

*"What did you tell yourself as you practiced?" he asked.*

*"I was skeptical of this working so I said to myself, 'I'm certain that this won't work. What was, was. Who am I trying to fool by thinking that it happened differently than it did?' "*

*"No wonder it didn't work," he said. "You aren't trying to fool anyone. You're not claiming that this upgraded way of behaving was what really happened. What you are doing is creating a new scene of how you would have wanted to act. This is a new picture that you want to use as a positive resource."*

*This made sense to me. I tried doing this again. This time I remained open and nonjudgmental. I found that it was extremely helpful and I've recommended this to many of my friends.*

# 26.

# BREATHING IN COURAGE

In my book *Happiness: Formulas, stories, and insights,* I mentioned how each breath we take is another opportunity to feel grateful to the Creator for giving us that breath. We can also utilize breathing as a tool for increasing our level of courage.

You have the amazing ability to tell yourself, "With every breath I take, I am breathing in courage." As you breathe slowly and deeply, feel yourself taking in oxygen and at the same time feel yourself taking in more and more courage. Realize that oxygen is a gift to you from the Creator and so is the capacity to take the oxygen into your lungs and from there it is sent to all the cells of your body. This is a magnificent and brilliant system. The Creator of the entire universe is All powerful. Allow your awareness of His power to empower you with the courage you need to accomplish all that you can in this world.

Repeat the word "courage" as you take each breath. By doing this consciously for a while, your brain will keep doing this on its own. You are building up an association between breathing and courage. Since you breathe several times each minute and you keep this up twenty-four hours a day, this is an awesome tool for consistently building up your levels of courage.

If you ever need courage for a specific action you want to take, as you breathe visualize yourself breathing in courage. This will give you the courage you need. Do this lightly and gently. The more frequently you do this, the easier it will become.

*I was so far away from having courage that I knew there was no way that I could take just a few actions and all of a sudden I would become courageous. When courage was needed, people would often tell me, "Just do it!" I know that this works for many people. They just do it without a fuss. But I can't just do it. I feel that something stronger than me is holding me back.*

*I was very grateful when someone told me to breathe in courage. Since I plan to be breathing every day throughout the day, utilizing breathing as a means of increasing courage is a way that I can increase my courage level at my own pace.*

*When I have to make a telephone call that I find difficult, I sit near the telephone and repeat to myself, "Every breath I take is giving me more and more courage. Every breath I take is giving me more and more courage."*

*The length of time this takes to work for me varies. The more diffi-cult I find a specific telephone call, the more time I need to spend on breathing in courage. But I know that as long as I keep breathing it's just a matter of time until I increase my level of courage to the degree that I can do and say things that I previously used to feel I wouldn't be able to do or say.*

# 27.

# THE ULTIMATE PHRASE: "THERE IS NONE BESIDE HIM"

Three Hebrew words that will elevate one's life are *"ein ode milvado"* ("There is none beside Him") (*Deuteronomy* 4:35). This expresses the realization that there is no intrinsic power in all of creation other than the Creator. Nothing that exists has existence without His will. Rabbi Chaim of Volozhin wrote that when one meditates on these three words, one will be saved from all types of negative forces. When one internalizes the message of these three words, they are the source of invincible courage.

When Rabbi Yitzchok Zev Soloveitchik, the Brisker Rav, was in dangerous situations during World War II, he focused totally on these three words. He had a remarkable escape which he attributed to the power of the awareness that the only thing in the entire universe that exists is the A-mighty.

As you practice meditating on these three words and feel their meaning, you will find all stress and tension melting away. Repeat these words slowly. It helps to breathe slowly and deeply as you do.

As soon as you experience stress, anxiety, worry, or fears, let that serve as a cue to begin focusing on *ein ode milvado*. Some people have signs with these words. Others use them as screensavers for their computers.

*I had to deal with an angry bureaucrat for a minor infraction of some rules. Whether or not he would give me a large fine was totally up to his discretion. I meditated on* ein ode milvado *while I waited for him. And I kept this up when he interrupted our conversation to speak on the telephone. This helped me stay in a centered state. Things did work out the way I was hoping. But even if they had not, I still gained by internalizing this message on a deeper level.*

*When I was a young child and was afraid of the dark or of scary dreams, my parents would suggest that I repeat the words* ein ode milvado. *At first they would serenely repeat these words to me over and over in a very soothing voice. As I grew older these words have consistently been a source of inspiration and serenity.*

*Living in Israel, I sometimes come into the vicinity of a* cheifetz chashud — *an object suspected of containing an explosive device. Whenever I am in the vicinity of such an object, I meditate on* ein ode milvado. *These incidents increase my consciousness of G-d.*

# 28.

# EVERY SITUATION IS NEW

No situation is exactly like any other situation. Every situation is new. Therefore even if you have not acted with courage in a past situation, you presently have the capacity to make new choices when new situations arise.

We each change all the time, either slightly or considerably. The new situations that arise are always faced by a you that is more advanced in various ways than at any time in the past when you were faced with a similar situation. Let this thought strengthen you in your ability to have more courage than you ever did before.

One difference in any situation after you read this book is that now you are facing that situation with the knowledge you have gained from reading about courage. Even if you knew all that is written in this book before you read it, reading it now will reinforce the ideas and techniques you need to act with courage. The same applies after each reading of this book. You will always have more inner resources of courage after each review. You will be more aware of your own acts of courage. You will be more aware of the acts of courage of others that automatically become part of your own mental library.

You might find yourself being able to experience courage when interacting with certain people and not with others. Some people for whom this is true tend to tell themselves, "With this or that person I just don't have courage." But even with the same person, both of you are different in some ways every time you encounter each other. This is true even if the last time you saw that person was the day before or a few hours earlier. All the more so if it was a week ago, a month ago, or a year ago. Realizing that every situation is new can help you have more courage with someone even if this will be the first time in your life that you will experience courage with that person.

*If I ever felt intimidated by someone, every time I would see that person I would say to myself, "Here is a person I can't be assertive with." I would repeat the old pattern of avoidance or acting submissively. When I heard of the idea that each encounter is a brand new situation, I was skeptical as to how this would help me.*

*I kept this in mind, however. There was a person who was very brilliant with whom I would have liked to discuss some issues. I've always felt that here is a person I couldn't approach. I watched other people approach him and speak to him. And of course he didn't bite their heads off.*

*The next time I saw that person I said to myself, "I'm now differ-ent from before and this situation is new. Now I have carefully observed how other people approach him." This newness enabled me to approach him and I've gained immensely from this person's knowledge and insights.*

*I've wanted a raise for a long time. I tried a few times and was refused. After that whenever I think of going over to the boss and ask-ing for a raise, I hear an inner voice saying to me, "You've tried already and you didn't get it. Trying again will probably get you nowhere once again."*

*Now that I am committed to looking at each situation as new, I realize that the next time I ask for a raise, the situation will be dif-ferent. I will have had more experience on this job. I will have greater skills and talents. I will be able to do things for the company that I wasn't able to do before. My options will be expanded. I still need to wait for the right time. But I no longer allow a past refusal to prevent me from having the courage to try again.*

# 29

# JUST FOR TODAY

"Just for today" is a well-known tool that enables people to have a positive trait, state, or way of being one day at a time. Let the power of this concept work for you one day at a time.

Anyone can be kind, joyous, centered, or courageous for just one day. So if someone feels that it is hard for him to be kind all the time, let him be kind "just for today." If someone feels that it is hard for him to be joyous all the time, let him be joyous "just for today." If someone feels it is hard for him to be centered all the time, let him be centered "just for today." And if you do not feel that you can be courageous all the time, speak and act with courage "just for today."

*My self-image used to be that I lacked courage. Objective outsiders often told me, "You have a lot of courage." But this didn't ring totally true to me. Yes, it was true I frequently said things that took courage to say. And I have done a number of things that many others would be* too intimidated to do. But when it came to my self-concept, I viewed myself as a person who lacked courage.

Someone told me that my self-image reminded him of a statement he once saw quoted in The New York Times. A man with a fortune of nearly $900 million said, "You see these young guys worth $3 – $4 billion and you think to yourself, 'What have I done wrong?' "

Most people with even $100 million would consider themselves wealthy. But this person's self-image was based on his comparing himself with superwealthy people. Even though he had enough money to buy all that a normal human being would ever need his entire life, he viewed himself as financially deficient. So, too, I viewed myself as lacking courage even though I had a sufficient amount.

This made sense to me intellectually. But emotionally I still felt deficient when I asked myself, "Are you really a courageous person?"

What finally transformed me was the "just for today" tool. Based on what was suggested to me, I kept telling myself, "I only need courage just for today." Yes, I had the self-image of being able to have courage for just one day. And ever since, I have found that this is all the courage I need to handle life one day at a time.

I read about a prisoner of war who sustained his courage one day at a time. He didn't know how long he would be imprisoned and his conditions were unimaginably miserable. Living in captivity, he needed to act totally submissive to his captors. The actual suffering was multiplied by the psychological torment of not knowing how long he would have to endure the horrific misery.

*"What kept me going," he said, "was the thought that I only need to master enough courage and strength for one day. From the moment I woke up in the morning, I knew that I only have to cope "just for today."*

*Since my life challenges are much lighter than this person's, I realized that having courage "just for today," would give me the inner strength I needed.*

# 30.

# ACCEPTING THE WORST

When you mentally prepare yourself to accept the worst, you will find it easier to handle a difficult reality that is not as bad as the scenario you already have accepted.

This can be especially effective when you humorously exaggerate the potentially negative outcome. For example, you need to ask a very stern person for someone's telephone number. You find this person intimidating and find it difficult to ask him if he knows the number you need. Most likely if the person knows the number by heart or has it written down, he will tell it to you. The actual worst-case scenario is usually that he will say in a slightly annoyed tone of voice, "No, I don't have the number." And a little worse than that might be, "Why in the world would you assume that I have the number?" Not the most pleasant thing, but not really devastating.

To build up your ability to approach this person, you might make a picture of him yelling and shouting at the top of his lungs, "How dare you have the extreme insolence of asking such an important personage like me for a telephone number? You are such a nothing and I'm such a V.I.P. Do you think that I work as an operator for the telephone company? Never ask me such questions again!"

Mentally run this scene over and over again. As you do, you can make the scene even a bit more ridiculous. Have the person jump up and down in a rage and fury as he says these things to you. When you actually ask him for the telephone number, you will find the reality a breeze.

*I used to be very nervous about speaking in public. I imagined that people would be critical of what I had to say. Some people might already know the material. Others would disagree. Yet others would be bored.*

*I spoke to someone who seemed to love speaking in public. He told me that when he gets up to speak, he tells himself, "If even one person will gain from what I have to say, I consider all my efforts worthwhile."*

*What helped him in the beginning was that he imagined the worst. He mentally saw everyone standing up and jeering him. He saw them clapping in unison, shouting, "Get out of here. Get out of here."*

*When he actually walked into a room where he was about to speak, he would nod and smile, and many smiled back. He laughs every time he thinks of the mental pictures he used to envision.*

# 31

# BE A TECHNIQUE COLLECTOR

Many people have developed techniques to enable themselves to act with courage. Whenever you hear or read about a helpful courage-increasing technique, add it to your mental library. Some people have no need for these techniques. They either automatically have courage or just psyche themselves up and immediately experience courage. For those who benefit from techniques here are some that have proven helpful to others:

- "I see myself as an infant whom the Creator blessed with courage. I also see myself as coming from a long line of courageous ancestors. I have inherited courage and this is an integral part of me."

- "I imagine a powerful invisible shield surrounding me. This gives me a feeling of emotional invincibility towards anything negative said to me."

- "I see myself as a gigantic lion or leopard. I do this based on the statement of Yehudah, the son of Teima, in *Ethics of the Fathers* 5:23. The lion or leopard is the size of a tall building.

The power I feel is incredible. This gives me the strength to interact well with the most frightening people. Of course, I realize that I am still a vulnerable normal human being, so I don't use this to take foolish risks. But it does help me to overcome unnecessary feelings of intimidation."

- "When I find it difficult to speak to someone, I don't look him straight in the eye. Rather I focus on a spot slightly above his eyes. Then I don't feel as nervous. At times, I will look for pimples, warts, blemishes, even freckles on the person's face. This enables me to look at him as an equal."

- "When I need to speak to people who intimidate me, I imagine that they are little infants crying. This makes it easier for me to speak up."

- "I mentally go to a peaceful garden. The serene feelings of the garden gives me the strength to increase my level of courage."

- "I allow myself to hear an inner voice as if it were coming from the outside telling me, 'You have now been given the gift of courage.'"

- "I see myself in a circle of excellence. I see the floor of this circle as being half silver and half gold. This circle is a place of total courage. I imagine that the most courageous people of all times entered this circle. They all left a copy of their own courage. Whenever I need more courage, I see myself entering this circle where I soon experience the courage I need."

- "I put the palm of my hand on my forehead and I feel the courage that is inside my brain cells becoming activated. At times I do this by putting one hand on my forehead and the other hand on my neck."
- "I see a special laser machine. The laser radiates beams of courage. Whenever I need a refill of courage, I imagine myself being in front of this machine. This works for me with amazing speed."
- "I imagine myself as being full of a blue liquid that represents courage."
- "As I walk down the street I repeat to myself, 'With each and every step that I take, I am getting more and more courage.'"
- "I visualize myself standing in front of myself in a state of intense and total courage and empowerment. I make this picture large and vivid and close. As I look at the picture, I feel myself breathing the way I would breath with total courage. I see the look of joyous empowerment and courage on my face and in my posture. I hear myself speaking with tremendous courage. Then I take this picture and turn it into a small dot. I have the dot zoom forth into a large and close vivid picture of courage. I redo this a number of times until I can take the dot with me wherever I go and have it blossom into a powerful image of myself with courage. Then I take the courageous image of myself and put it into the palm of my left hand. I multiply this picture into many

thousands of pictures, even a million of them. I see them forming a long, long line. Then I take these pictures and have them form concentric circles all around me. When I look up, I see thousands of pictures of myself being courageous. When I look behind me, I see thousands of pictures of myself being courageous. These pictures form a high wall and ceiling. Behind me and in front of me all I see is myself being courageous. I repeat this frequently. This also helps me experience greater joy and any other worthwhile inner resource."

# 32.

# COURAGE AND HUMILITY

umility makes it easier to have courage. Humility frees you from worrying about how others perceive you. You have less of a need to make a good impression on people, so you are more open to learn new things. You do not mind if people see that you are imperfect or that you are not as skilled or talented as you would like to be. An arrogant or conceited person always needs to appear to be perfect, to be highly skilled and talented. This creates tension and anxiety. The truly humble person is calmer and more relaxed.

Humility frees a person from worrying about whether people praise him or insult him. When someone reaches this level of humility which takes much reflection and study, he will find it relatively easy to do what others find difficult. For example, why are people afraid to ask questions? They are afraid someone will think they are not intelligent if they ask a silly question or one to which they should have known the answer. For someone with humility, this is not a concern.

Therefore they find it easy to ask questions.

A person with humility does not compete with others for glory, fame, honor, or approval. Therefore he is not apprehensive about taking any kind of test. If he does poorly, he views it as feedback for what he knows and does not know. He might enter various forms of competition for practical purposes, but his self-image is still that he is created in the A-mighty's image and he is a child of the Creator. Win or lose this remains his self-image. No victory could increase his sense of self-worth. A victory of any kind is trivial compared to the reality he lives with about who he is. And a defeat cannot detract from his being created in the A-mighty's image.

Humility and a low self-image are worlds apart. A person with genuine humility realizes that His total value is exactly what the Creator has given to him and this is immense. A person with low self-esteem lacks positive feelings about himself. A person with genuine humility is a happy person. A person with a low self-image is not. A person with genuine humility is an active doer. A person with a low self-image is not. A person with genuine humility is serene. A person with a low self-image is not. A person with genuine humility has courage. A person with a low self-image lacks it.

Someone who is arrogant or conceited feels a need for courage because he needs others to think that he is courageous in addition to all his other virtues. So added to all his other concerns he feels a strong need to seem brave at all times.

Humility frees a person from this. He has courage and does not feel a need to prove this to anyone else

*I used to think that humility was the opposite of courage. I thought that someone who is courageous would walk around radiating total confidence and strength. The first time someone told me that humility increases courage, I argued with him. But it was suggested to me, "Observe the people you feel are the most open to learn new things. Observe which people are not afraid of asking clarification questions. Observe which people are the most open to listen to constructive criticism. Observe which people are the least affected by insults." I did. And I too agree that humility increases confidence. Whenever I see that I lack courage, the first thing I now say to myself is, "This is feedback that I need to upgrade my level of humility."*

# 33.

# A COURAGE COACH

Ultimately any courage you have is within you. You can choose to access your own courage this very moment. A coach for courage is not a prerequisite. But most people would gain from having someone who can help them increase their level of courage.

A coach might be an expert or even someone who is working on beginning stages of this trait. Just knowing that you can share your successes can often make it easier for you. While you are in the midst of a difficult situation, having in mind that your coach will be proud of your progress can serve as a strong motivator. If you ever feel that you are not making as much progress as you would have wished, your coach can encourage you.

Make certain to find someone who inspires you and who believes in your ability to achieve greater levels of courage. If you feel that a certain coach is excessively critical and you find yourself not being open with the reality of your situation, try to muster up enough courage to tell this coach how you would want to be spoken to. Ask the coach to focus on progress and positive patterns of encouragement. If the coach agrees to this, great. If not, have the courage to tell that coach, "At the present I feel that I need a different approach. If you aren't open to this, then I will try to find someone whose approach is more similar to the one that I feel I need." If you are able to do this, this coach has helped you more than you might have thought.

When you build up your own courage, you will be able to serve as a coach to others. Some of the best courage coaches are those who had to struggle to attain the courage they now have. Since it did not come easily to them, they know what it is like to lack the courage to do what others consider easy. If you do not yet have the courage you would like, let the knowledge that you will inevitably be able to help others serve as a further motivating factor for you to increase your own courage.

*I am grateful to my parents for continually serving as my courage coaches. I am told that I was much more shy and timid than most children. I remember when I was about 4 years old and a new child came to our kindergarten. My mother told me to go out of my way to be friendly with that child. My mother knew that it was hard for me to approach strangers. So she said to me, "It's an important good deed to be friendly to another boy who is new to your school. I know it's hard for you, but force yourself to do it anyway." I remember how proud my grandmother was when I told her, "Today in kindergarten there was a new boy. I was friendly to him even though it was hard for me."*

I lacked courage, but I didn't feel like sharing this with anyone else. Someone changed my life by taking the initiative to approach me and say, "I hope that I'm not being too forward. But I feel that you are very much the way I was when I was your age. I used to be very unassertive and would shy away from situations that took courage. Over the years, I've built up my courage beyond what I believed I could. If you will allow me, I will share with you some of the lessons that I have learned. If someone were to have come over to me, they would have saved me much time and distress."

I was greatly impressed with this person's candor and kindness. The way he approached me with regard to increasing courage appealed to me. When I asked him how I could repay him, he replied, "Just be on the lookout for other people you can help in this area."

# 34.

# STUDENTS OF NACHSHON

At the splitting of the Red Sea, the first one to jump into the water was Nachshon, the son of Aminadav, from the tribe of Judah. Everyone was terrified. The Egyptians were pursuing the Israelites with the Red Sea putting a halt to their forward progress. People differed about whether it was preferable to fight the Egyptians or to return to slavery. Nachshon had the courage to be the first to go forward. He led the way and others followed.

The great sage Hillel tells us to be a student of Aaron, the older brother of Moses, who became the first High Priest (*Ethics of the Fathers* 1:11). Aaron loved and pursued peace. He loved people and brought them to Torah. This concept of being a student of someone who lived many years ago applies to the courage of Nachshon. What qualifies you to be a student of Nachshon? The willingness to go first.

When a speaker completes his lecture and asks for questions, often there is silence. But once the first question is asked, others are apt to ask their questions. It can take courage to be the first to open a discussion.

When a new school opens, it can be scary to be among the first to attend. One can never be certain that it will succeed. If you feel the school is for you, be a student of Nachshon and be the first.

Be careful to weigh the entire picture of a new situation. There are many projects, institutions, and organizations that do not turn out the way their promoters claim they will. You yourself might be overly optimistic about a plan of yours. It is usually worthwhile to get feedback from people with much life experience to hear what they have to say about the matter. But there have been many instances when almost everyone told someone, "I am 100- percent positive that this won't work out." The visionary, pioneer, or entrepreneur went forward anyway and was immensely successful.

Even if you are not the actual first, joining an existing project, organization, or institution in its early stages is also an aspect of having the courage of Nachshon. As there is still a risk factor when you join, you will be increasing your level of courage.

*There was an appeal made to raise funds for a worthy cause. There was an uncomfortable silence as no one wanted to be the first to make a pledge. My father raised his hand and offered a very generous amount. Others followed by pledging more than they usually would.*

*On the way home, my father said to me, "I like to be the first one to make a pledge when I feel that something is worthwhile. I know that if I start off with a large amount, others will also give more than usual. I appreciate the mitzvah of influencing others to do good deeds."*

# 35

# HOW OTHERS VIEW YOU

When we are young, the way we are viewed by others has a major effect on our character and personality. Whether we view ourselves as intelligent or not, whether we view ourselves as kind or selfish, whether we view ourselves as skilled and talented or not, will be greatly effected by the messages we hear from parents, siblings, other relatives, friends, teachers, and the many individuals we encounter.

As we grow older, we can become more independent. We can free ourselves from limiting views of others and develop our own picture of ourselves. We are subjective about ourselves and therefore we might view ourselves as having more of a positive trait than we actually do, or we might view ourselves as having less. Therefore, to gain an accurate picture of ourselves, we need the feedback of reliable people.

But other people are limited in how they view us. You might have much more courage than others realize. No mortal knows your struggles, your difficulties, your challenges, the extent of your suffering and pain, and your worries. These are factors that increase the level of courage that you might experience without it being realized. Even if it is realized, it will not be to its fullest extent. So even if others do not see you as having high levels of courage, you actually do.

Others cannot know the full extent of your goals, your aspirations, your dreams, your visions, your wishes, your hopes, and your prayers. These can be much more courageous than anyone else might imagine. Here it is important to have a mixture of present reality with believing that the A-mighty can enable you to accomplish, do, and be so much more than anyone can know.

To summarize, utilize the feedback of others to realize how they see you. This can help you be more aware of your blind spots. But never allow the view of any human being to limit you needlessly. Regardless of how you are at any given moment, the Creator can help you to realize greatness of character. He will send you opportunities that challenge you and enable you to consistently become more than you were before.

*Some people appear to others to have much more courage than they actually experience. With me, it's the opposite. On the outside, I often appear to be meek and timid. On the inside, I have the total courage of my beliefs and convictions. I am willing to do whatever it takes and am willing to take risks to do the will of Hashem. I don't feel a need to boast or to appear powerful to others. As a child, I was afraid of* strangers, of dogs, and possible injury. I still have a few phobias in inconsequential areas. This makes me appear to some people as if I lack courage. Of course, I do lack it in some ways. But my view of myself as having courage has enabled me to accomplish more than I ever thought I would.

I am very grateful to my parents for giving me the gift of courage. They would frequently point out to me, "That took courage," when I did new things. If other children did something wrong and I didn't join them, my father or mother would say, "You have just increased your courage." Their positive messages have reverberated in my mind hundreds of times. Even as an adult when I do something that takes courage, I hear their voices telling me, "That took courage," and "You have just increased your courage."

# 36.

# IT'S NORMAL TO BE SCARED AT TIMES

*When I was younger it was very important for me to build up a reputation for myself that I wasn't afraid of anybody or anything. But the reality was that at times I was afraid. I did everything I could to hide my fear from everyone else. This just made it much more difficult for me. I was afraid that if I would show fear even one time, people would consider me to be cowardly. I guess that was my biggest fear.*

*What helped me greatly was that there was someone I respected. He was brave, but still careful not to do anything that was needlessly risky.*

*Once I asked him, "Are you ever scared of anything?"*

*"Plenty of times," he replied.*

*"I assume that you try to hide it from others," I commented.*

*"Why should I?" he answered. "I don't claim to be superhuman. I'm a normal human being. We are all vulnerable in many ways. I'm not afraid of anyone being aware of my fear of injury in a dangerous situation. I even have a couple of irrational phobias. I'd like to overcome them. But I don't have any reason to keep this a secret."*

*Now I respected him even more. He had the courage to acknowledge that he was vulnerable. I followed his example, and didn't try to hide my fears. Shortly afterwards, I had an important interview. On the way to the interview I bumped into a friend of mine. In the old days I would have forced myself to look totally relaxed and comfortable, but not this time.*

*"You look nervous," my friend said to me.*

*"I am," I answered. "I have an important interview."*

*"That's how I feel when I have an important interview. I wish you great success," he said to me.*

*I was astounded beyond words. "And this is what I've been afraid of my entire life!" I said to myself.*

If you are a normal human being, you will be fearful some of the time. Every young child has fears. As we get older we learn to differentiate between what is a real danger and what is not. It is a healthy human reaction to feel anxiety when our life or well-being is in danger. This anxiety is a warning signal to be careful and to do what needs to be done to protect yourself.

Everyone has phobias in some form or other. These are fears that are exaggerated. We are not actually in any danger, but we feel frightened. Many people are afraid of mice. While mice will almost never bite or scratch a person, they elicit fear. The same is true with regard to snakes, even harmless ones. Many people are afraid to speak in public, and are nervous when they do. Some people are afraid of rejection or failure or of making mistakes. These types of fears can be overcome, but they are normal in the sense that the vast majority of people will possess them in some way.

You do not have to make a public announcement of your fears. But by not hiding them, you will find them easier to deal with.

"Aren't there times when it's preferable to hide one's fears?" is a standard question.

"Yes, there are," is the answer. Parents might feel a need to hide their fears of their financial situation from their children so the children will not worry needlessly. Teachers might want to hide their fears from students so the students will be more at ease. When dealing with a bully, it is best to avoid showing external signs of fear even though the inner feelings are appropriate. A policeman told me, "Regardless of any fear I may inwardly experience, I can never show a suspect that I feel apprehensive."

If you know that someone might tease you for being frightened of something that is not dangerous, you might want to hide your fears. But in these types of situations, perhaps you might use this as an opportunity to overcome your fear of being teased. No one likes to be teased and it is a violation of Torah law to cause distress by teasing. But if someone who teases you will not stop even though you ask respectfully, your best move would be to learn how to transcend this fear.

# 37.
# TAKE THE INITIATIVE

"If you have something negative about yourself that you wish to share with others, take the initiative to say it right away at the beginning" (*Bava Kamma* 92b). This is an effective tool to use when it comes to overcoming needless fears of other people.

If you want to ask a question and are afraid that someone will become angry at you, at times it is worthwhile to say, "I would like to ask you a question, but I am afraid to ask."

The majority of people will reply, "You don't need to be afraid. Feel free to ask."

If you need to ask someone a favor and are afraid to ask, you might find it helpful to say, "I would like to ask a favor of you, but I am afraid to ask."

You cannot expect people to make a blind commitment, but they will usually be open to allow you to ask them.

If you are intimidated about asking someone to give a donation to a charitable cause, you might say, "I would like to ask you if you would be interested in donating to a very worthwhile cause, but I am afraid to ask."

Kindhearted and generous people will say something like, "If it's a worthy cause I would like to hear about it." Or, they might apologize to you, "I'm sorry. I would love to help out but right now I'm overextended." Either way, you will be increasing your level of courage.

*I attended a sales seminar. The person giving the seminar said that one of the biggest problems people who are trying to succeed in sales have is that they have fears of asking for things. This is almost universal for people who are just beginning. Even with people who have been in the field for a long time, many feel anxious about various aspects of selling.*

*The person giving the seminar would ask members of the audience, "What are you most afraid to do?"*

*A common fear is being afraid to ask for the sale. Some people get around this by asking, "Would you like one or two?" or, "Would you want to take this now or do you want it delivered?"*

*This master salesman suggested, "I know this is going to sound a bit strange. But if you are afraid of something, tell the potential customer right away. For example you can say, 'I love the product (or service) that I sell. I'm very enthusiastic about it. I will be glad to tell you all about it. But I have a problem. Do you know what my problem is? I am afraid to ask you to buy it. I know that you will gain, but I find it too difficult to ask you for your money. So I will describe my product (or service) and if you are interested in buying it, please raise your hand. Then I will know you want it.' "*

*He guaranteed the audience that if they would put this into practice, they would only have to use this a few times. After doing this, you will find that your fears disappear.*

*I applied this and found that it worked for me in a number of diverse situations.*

# 38

# "I CAN'T" VERSUS "NOT YET"

C ompare these two patterns. The first is: "I can't."

- "I can't ask questions when I don't understand something."
- "I can't ask this person to speak to me respectfully."
- "I can't ask for a raise."
- "I can't raise funds for this worthy cause."
- "I can't tell this person to stop smoking."

Now let us analyze the "not yet" pattern:

- "I do not yet have the courage to ask people for what I want."
- "I do not yet have the courage to ask questions when I do not understand something."
- "I do not yet have the courage to ask this person to speak to me respectfully."

- "I do not yet have the courage to ask for a raise."
- "I do not yet have the courage to raise funds for this worthy cause."
- "I do not yet have the courage to tell this person to stop smoking."

When you say, "I can't," you are making a claim that a certain way of speaking or action is impossible. It is impossible to start flying just by waving your hands. It is impossible to swim across the Atlantic Ocean without stopping. It is impossible to climb Mount Everest in two hours. But it is possible to speak up, to ask questions, to ask for donations, to ask someone if he would be interested in buying something, and to try to influence someone in a positive way.

When you say, "I do not yet have the courage to do this or that," you are acknowledging that you have the potential to do this. All that is needed is more courage than you are experiencing this moment. This opens up an entire world of new possibilities.

*I used to think that I couldn't learn a foreign language. I repeated this idea over and over again. It seemed to me to be an absolute fact. Someone who offered to teach me that language said to me, "I know you can do it. But you don't yet have the courage to practice over and over. You don't yet have the courage to ask someone to make you a tape that you can learn from. You don't yet have the courage to keep asking people many times how to say things and what specific words mean. As soon as you acquire this courage, you will be able to succeed. And I'm certain that you actually have this courage deep inside. Claim it and it's yours." This encouragement moved me and now I can communicate fairly well in a language I never thought I could know.*

# 39.

# ASKING FOR FORGIVENESS

For some people the most difficult thing in the world is to ask for forgiveness. And this can come from two opposite behavior patterns. On one hand, there is the person who feels that he never does anything wrong. If he gets into a quarrel it is always the other party's fault. If someone feels bad about something he said or did, he blames the other person for choosing to feel that way. It is that person's fault for being so sensitive. If he says or does something in anger, regardless of what it is, it is always the fault of the person who caused him to become angry. This person lacks the courage to take an objective look at his words and actions. This person fails to take responsibility for what he has done wrong.

On the other hand, there are people who feel terribly guilty whenever they cause someone else distress or pain in any way. They find it very difficult to ask for forgiveness because they feel so embarrassed and ashamed for saying or doing something they should not have said or done. They would love to ask for forgiveness, but they are afraid of the reaction of the other person. Maybe that person will say something in hurt or in anger that they will find too devastating to hear.

More courage is needed for people who fit into either category. For those who feel they never hurt anyone, if other people feel that they do, they probably do. They might not have had the intention to hurt someone, but since they did, they need the courage to say, "I am sorry that I caused you pain. Please forgive me." And for those who are embarrassed to ask for forgiveness, they will be building up their courage by overcoming that embarrassment. They need the courage to say, "I am sorry that I caused you pain. Please forgive me."

If you find it difficult to ask for forgiveness, visualize yourself asking for forgiveness. Mentally see yourself approaching someone and saying, "I am sorry that I caused you pain. Please forgive me." Play this picture in your mind over and over again. Feel a sense of strength and release on being able to do this.

Each time you ask for forgiveness and find it difficult, you are building up your inner resource of courage.

Just as it takes courage to ask for forgiveness, it can take courage to forgive. There are instances when a person feels so hurt that he is not ready yet to forgive. Then you can say, "I wish that I would be able to sincerely say that I forgive you. But as of yet I can't. Please ask me again in a week (two weeks, a month). Hopefully, I'll be able to forgive you then." Here, too, when you view forgiving someone as an act of courage, you will have added motivation to forgive.

*I knew someone who would always be the first to ask for forgiveness from others. I asked him, "Don't you find this difficult?"*

*"In the beginning I did," he replied. "But after a number of times, it has become much easier. Even so, there are times when I find it extremely difficult. I mentally intensify my level of courage and force myself to ask. I realize that the more difficult it is, the more I gain spiritually and emotionally. There are some situations when people are upset with me that I feel they have no justification for blaming me. Nevertheless, since they do blame me, I am a cause of their pain. It's more important for me to help people out of their pain than to stubbornly claim that I don't need to ask them for forgiveness."*

*There was someone who kept refusing to forgive me for my having caused him pain. I felt awful about this and asked forgiveness several times. I finally realized that this person refuses to forgive others in order to exercise power over them. His refusal to forgive comes from a manipulative place. At first I didn't have the courage to tell him what I thought. But then I decided to speak respectfully to him and tell him my thoughts.*

*"I feel that I am asking your forgiveness sincerely," I said to him. "I feel that you have an underlying reason for not forgiving me. This is your choice. I will be willing to ask you again, if the reason you find it difficult to forgive is because you are so hurt. But if you are just refusing to forgive for the power you feel, I suggest that you work on*

*your willingness to forgive."*

*While the person didn't explicitly acknowledge the validity of what I said, I could tell that my words had an effect. The next time I encountered that person, he said, "I forgive you."*

*For over fifteen years I felt that a very distinguished Torah scholar had a complaint against me. He never said anything explicitly to this effect, but I felt certain that he was disappointed and upset with me. I tried to avoid him out of feelings of discomfort. I kept thinking that I have an obligation to ask his forgiveness. It was too difficult for me to go by myself so I asked an older friend if he would accompany me and even speak for me.*

*"I don't have any complaints against you," the scholar said in a reassuring voice. "If, however, you feel you need my forgiveness, I forgive you a million times."*

*I felt as if a mountain was lifted from me. I still wasn't certain whether I had been making a mountain out of a molehill, or whether he really had been upset by me. Either way, having the courage to finally ask for forgiveness was a milestone for me. And I can't imagine any greater relief than hearing that he forgave me so wholeheartedly.*

# 40.

# "DO I HAVE A RIGHT TO SAY THIS?"

One of the most effective tools to gain assertiveness is to ask yourself the question, "Do I have a right to say this?" Whenever the answer is, "Yes," then you do not need to refrain from saying what you would like to say.

People who are highly assertive are aware of their rights. Such people will say:

- "I have a right to ask a question now."
- "I have a right to return this item to the store."
- "I have a right to ask to be spoken to politely and with respect."
- "I have a right to say that I am too busy to do this now."
- "I have a right to ask people to speak more quietly."
- "I have a right to ask people for directions."
- "I have a right to ask for my rights."

People who are not yet assertive need to increase their realization that they have the same rights as every other person on our planet. There is no special committee that doles out the rights listed above and there are people who just were not waiting in the right line, or if they were, the right to rights ran out.

If you are not certain whether you really do have the rights listed above and similar rights, think of someone whose opinion you can ask. Some people who somehow feel that they do not have these rights might hesitate to ask anyone else. But as soon as they view their hesitation to speak up as a feeling of lacking rights, they will realize it is obvious they have these rights. There is no need to consult anyone to receive a special gift of these rights. They were yours the moment you became a member of the human race.

*I used to be one of the most unassertive people you will ever meet. I wouldn't ask people questions unless I was absolutely forced to by extreme circumstances. I didn't have a clear reason why I was the way I am. I was envious of people who had no trouble speaking up whenever they felt like it. For me, even when I did speak up, I experienced strong anxiety and it always took me a while to calm down again.*

*"What is the difference in the way I look at things and the way assertive people look at things?" I asked myself. Before I asked this question, I would just say that it's a matter of personality. Some people have a personality of being assertive and some don't. And I'm just one of those people who have an unassertive personality. But I read that every single pattern we have can be altered. We need to model the*

way of thinking and acting of people who are able to do things that we can't yet do.

I interviewed people I considered to be masters of assertiveness. A sentence that I heard from a few of them was, "I have a right to speak up." That was it. They felt they had a right to speak up. I was always worried, "Maybe I will be bothering this person." "Maybe this person will become irritated or angry." "Maybe this person will be too busy to answer me." When I asked assertive people about my concerns they said something to the effect of, "I have a right to try. I can't control how people will respond to me. But as long as I speak respectfully to people, there is no valid reason why I shouldn't ask for my basic rights."

Once I realized that it was all right for me to speak up, I found it much easier than I had imagined.

# 41.

# THE COURAGE TO DISAGREE

- *"I am afraid that if I disagree with people, they will dislike me."*

- *"I am afraid that people will consider me difficult to get along with if I argue with what they say."*

- *"I associate disagreeing with being obnoxious."*

It can take courage to disagree with what others say. When you do disagree, be respectful of the person with whom you disagree. As is often said, "Disagree without being disagreeable." Do not make any put-down comments. For example, do not say anything similar to:

- "That's ridiculous. How could you say that?"

- "Only an idiot would think that way."

- "That was a stupid thing to say."

Rather, when you disagree, start with a statement such as:

- "It seems to me that…"
- "Let's explore the possibility of looking at it this way."
- "I may not be right, but at present I would say…"

When you disagree politely and respectfully, you will not be disliked, people will not consider you difficult to get along with, and no one will consider you obnoxious.

Be on the lookout for role models of people who disagree in a dignified manner. Listen to their tone of voice and the patterns of what they say.

You might find it easier to disagree if you ask permission, as it were, to disagree. For example, "Could I share with you the way I see things?" Not many people will consistently refuse to hear what you have to say.

Begin with an "agreement frame." That is, start off by acknowledging the points you agree on.

"I see that we agree about the basic issue. What I see differently is…"

"We both want to get along harmoniously. At the same time there is a point with which I seem to differ with what was said."

At times the point you do agree with is minor. Nonetheless begin with that rather than with your disagreement.

Every time you disagree respectfully, you are increasing your level of courage. This reframe will make it easier for you to state your opinion even if it is in the minority.

Have the courage not to disagree if you see that the person you disagree with will take it too personally or will get angry at you and nothing will be gained by your disagreeing.

*I work for a major international company where I am in middle management. At times before a business meeting, I speak to a number of people who will be attending and I pre-sell. That is, I present my position to them and see how they react. I find it very frustrating when people tell me before a meeting they will vote with my position, but don't. They frequently are too intimidated by a person with a stronger personality and vote against the position they had agreed to. I discussed this with an older individual and he advised me to include a booster shot of courage. I realized that this was missing. The people I work with are highly intelligent and competent. But when they lack courage, they aren't able to stand up to a position they feel is incorrect. I usually have the courage of my convictions. And now my goal is to help those people increase their own level of courage before we go into the meetings.*

# 42.

# HEARING CRITICISM

*"I love criticism. I can't wait for people to tell me what I'm doing wrong. It gives me great pleasure to be told my faults and mistakes. I go out of my way to meet people who will censure and admonish me. One of the most enjoyable aspects of living is having people in your life who will criticize you for every minor error and blunder."*

Think for a moment, "How many people do you know who could say the above statement with a straight face?" In *Ethics of the Fathers* (6:6), "loving criticism" is listed as number thirty-five of the forty-eight tools for acquiring Torah. Nevertheless, this is an extremely difficult level to attain. Until we get there, we need courage to listen to criticism. The more you dislike it, the more courage it takes to listen as objectively as you can.

There are a number of defensive patterns that are used when someone dislikes criticism. Here are some:

1. "You have the exact same faults that I do. In fact, you are really worse than I am. You have done such and such."

2. "I don't have those faults. You are totally wrong."

3. "Why don't you comment when I do something right? You only focus on what's wrong."

4. "I have to go now. Why do you always choose to bring up issues at the wrong time?"

5. "You said that I made six mistakes. It was only four. You always exaggerate and I've told you a million times that you should never do this again."

6. "This is my nature and I can't do anything about it. If you don't like it, it's your problem."

Let's look at this list from the viewpoint of courage:

1. The fact that this person does have the same faults does not negate the fact that you made a mistake or did something wrong. Have the courage to acknowledge your mistake.

2. Telling the criticizer that he is totally wrong might be correct. And if he is in error, it is appropriate to point it out. But if there is any validity in the comments, which is frequently the case, acknowledge those aspects of what he said that you know to be true. At times you might say, "I have to think it over. Until now I didn't realize this. I'll weigh what you say."

3. Is it accurate that the person never gives you positive feedback? If this is the reality, you might say, "You are correct about the present criticism. I would like to point

out that it would be much easier for me to listen to the negative feedback if you would also give me positive feedback." Some people find it difficult to ask for positive feedback. If this is difficult for you and you want it, then it would be yet another opportunity to increase your courage.

4. If the person does bring up the criticism at the wrong times, then have the courage to tell the person what would be the right time. If you are busy, then make the time. Listening to the criticism might be highly beneficial for you.

5. Criticizing the criticizer for a minor error in a basically correct statement is a smokescreen. This is especially so when the defensive approach is based on exaggeration.

6. Courage means that you try to change what can be changed. Anything based on the way we speak, what we say and how we say it, can be changed and upgraded. Anything based on actions that we do or do not do can be changed. It can be very difficult to change. We might have acted a certain way for a long time. Habit becomes second nature. But it can be changed by developing new habits. Every action you do in this direction increases your courage.

*I used to hate criticism. If someone criticized me on a specific issue, I viewed it as a total attack on my entire being. With some people, I would get angry and yell something back at them. With people I respected and couldn't express anger, I would become depressed. A teacher suggested that I view criticism as a tool for gaining more courage. My reaction towards any criticism was so negative that I didn't think I could change the way I reacted. But I did. Hearing criticism has not become my favorite pastime. But I do see it now as a way to increase courage. I have become more objective. To me this has been a highly effective reframe.*

# 43

# COURAGE OF "NO EXCUSES"

T he natural response when we are blamed is to give excuses. This was the response of Adam, the first man. He blamed Eve for his partaking of the forbidden fruit. When Eve was blamed, she blamed the Serpent. They both were partially right. Adam did have a reason to blame Eve. Eve did have a reason to blame the Serpent. But that did not justify their actions. They should have acknowledged that they were wrong and regretted what they did. They should have resolved and been committed never to do anything similar again.

It takes courage to say, "No excuses. I was wrong." Some people are terrified to say this – not because they are in situations when they need to be afraid of physical harm or financial loss, but because emotionally it is easier to give excuses or to blame someone else.

Why do so many people grow up with this phobia? Why is it so difficult to say, "No excuses. I was wrong"? Children are afraid that their parents will punish them if they do not offer an excuse. Students are afraid of their teachers' reactions if they do not give an excuse. Employees are afraid of their employers' reactions if they do not have an excuse. Husbands and wives are afraid of one another's reaction if they do not give an excuse.

If the excuse is a totally valid one, it is understandable and appropriate to mention it. The child did not clean up his room because he needed to study for a crucial test. After he finished studying, he intended to clean up. The student did not do his homework because he had intense pains yesterday evening and needed to check it out with a doctor. An employee was late for work because of a major traffic jam due to a horrible accident that closed down the only road. A husband or wife did not buy something because he/she had to take care of a matter that was clearly of a higher priority.

But when you did something that was wrong, or you forgot to do something you know you should have taken care of, get into the habit of responding, "No excuses. I was wrong." This will increase your sense of courage. This will prevent many arguments. This will enhance your integrity.

The difficulty of saying, "No excuses. I was wrong," only exists in the beginning. After saying this a number of times one will experience these words as empowering. It would be wrong to use this as a pseudorationalization for purposely doing something wrong. But when you are trying your best and still make a mistake, train yourself to say, "No excuses. I was wrong."

*I have many employees. I understand that it's humanly impossible for them never to make a mistake. Every human either forgets to do things or doesn't get around to it. But the most important characteristic to me in my employees is integrity and courage. Whenever I admonish one of my employees what I respect is when they respond, "No excuse. I was wrong."*

*I can't stand it if an employee starts by saying, "It wasn't my fault. It was his fault." or, "I'm not to blame. I was tired." What goes through my mind is, "Here we go again." If my employees would realize that this is what I want from them and that this would win them my respect, they would make an effort to respond, "No excuses. I was wrong."*

*I remember the day when someone I complained to about this said to me, "If your employees don't respond that way, it's your fault for not clarifying to them that this is what you want and respect."*

*My response was, "No excuses. I was wrong."*

*I saw that this was empowering to me. Then I found it easier to share my own experience with my employees. Now that this is the standard reply in our company we all gain. I am open to hear valid excuses. But the invalid ones have disappeared.*

# 44.
# LEARNING NEW THINGS

We each have new things that we are able to learn quickly, and other things that take us much longer. When we learn quickly, we usually feel good about ourselves and good about what we are learning. But when we try to learn something that takes us longer than we would like or longer than it takes others, we need courage.

The goal is to experience pleasure whenever you learn something new. The more you enjoy what you are learning, the easier it will be for you to remember it. When a person is anxious about what he is learning, the anxiety slows down the learning process. Have the courage to enjoy what you are learning.

Realize that your value as a person is a given. You are always a being who was created in the image of the Creator. You are always a child of the Creator. Even if it takes you longer than you would like to learn something, realize that this has nothing to do with your value as a person.

Part of the issue is fear of what other people will think. "People might think that I am slow," is what goes through many people's minds. When you master joy, kindness, and courage, you will be in great shape in life. The more joy you have, the less you worry what others think about you. When you focus on doing acts of kindness, your main concern is what you can do for others, and not on whether others consider you fast or slow. If you are concerned about other people thinking that you are slow, having the courage to transcend this increases your level of courage. This is of greater value than having people think that you are quick thinking.

*With regard to learning new things I would frequently say, "This is too hard for me." What I was claiming was that this was impossible for me to learn. But the reality was that I knew if I put in enough time to hear the ideas over and over again, I would eventually catch on. What I needed was the courage to ask people to repeat things. What I needed was the courage to ask people to wait so I could write down what they were saying. What I needed was the courage to ask people if I could tape what they were saying so I could repeat the segments I found difficult. What I needed was the persistence to review what I had written down and the literature that others suggested I read.*

*What increased my courage to learn new things was that I met someone who had been in school with me and was slower than I was. He had accomplished a great deal and had mastered a lot of information. I asked him how he did it. He told me, "Since I knew that I was slower than most of the other students in the class, I knew that I had to review what I learned more times than did the others. I enjoyed the entire process of reviewing since I knew that with each repetition I was gaining." This gave me the confidence to do the same and it has changed my life.*

*I viewed myself as shy and that's the way others viewed me. I did not ask questions when I didn't understand things. And I didn't take the initiative to find people to teach me. People who cared about me would quote the passage, "A bashful person cannot learn* (Ethics of the Fathers 2:6). *" This just increased my viewing myself as bashful.*

*I decided that if I were to fight my self-image of being shy, I probably wouldn't get very far. Instead, I decided to increase my ability to experience courage. Exactly because I was so shy, that's why for me it would be considered courageous to transcend the shyness that inhibited me. I continued to consider myself shy. It was courage that enabled me to accomplish that which I would have accomplished were I not shy.*

# 45.

# COURAGE TO LEARN FROM TRIAL AND ERROR

The greatest teacher in the world is known as: "trial and error." This has given more people more wisdom than any other teacher possibly could. "There is no greater wise person than someone with experience." This quote is cited by Rabbi Simcha Zissel of Kelm. What does it mean to have experience? It means that one has learned from trial and error. If everyone would get it right the first time, experience is not needed.

No one likes to make errors. Some people dread it. But that is the only way we can gain expertise. We can read about ideas in a book. We can receive instructions from teachers. But in order to really know how to do something well we need to take action. And every time we choose a particular action we might be making a mistake.

Having the courage to try even though you might make a mistake enables you to learn from trial and error. This is a valuable reframe. Instead of becoming overly frustrated or discouraged when you make a mistake, realize that now you are becoming wiser. Now that you know what does not work, you are a step closer to finding out what does work. If you would have known what the correct action was before you took the erroneous one, you certainly would have chosen it. So trial and error was essential for you.

By remembering how much you have already learned from trial and error in the past, you will have a greater appreciation for its value. Take for example someone who is trying to learn a new computer program without having a clear instruction book. How can you tell which buttons accomplish what? You have to press them and see the response. If you need a certain response and are not sure of which button to push, you need to push a number of buttons and eventually trial and error teaches you what to do in the future. Since everyone who tries to do something similar knows that this is what will happen, the reaction is usually positive when the desired outcome happens. You do not feel that bad when you make an error, because unless a miracle happens it is impossible to get every move right the first time.

Think about what you would gain from increased courage to learn from trial and error. In certain fields such as medical surgery an error might be fatal. If an expert is available, one should not venture to try without the most thorough training. But in the vast majority of situations errors can be rectified. Your reaction to errors is a matter of the way you subjectively reframe them. Realizing that you are increasing your courage by learning from trial and error will give you the encouragement you need.

*I wanted to learn a new language but I was afraid that I would mispronounce words, use the wrong words, and my grammar would be improper. I avoided speaking in that language as much as I could. Someone I knew finally asked me why I didn't practice conversing with people for whom that language was their native tongue.*

*"I feel embarrassed knowing that I will make many mistakes," I replied.*

*"That's all the more reason you should practice speaking that language," he told me.*

*"For you, it's not only a matter of learning the language. You will be increasing your level of courage every time you speak. Native speakers will be able to point out the correct way to pronounce words and when the grammar is way off they are likely to tell you the proper usage. If you use the wrong words, they will point out the right words to use. You will be increasing your ability to learn from trial and error and this will help you gain in more ways than you can yet know."*

*Looking back, I see how right he was.*

# 46.

# ILLNESS: A COURAGE SEMINAR

verything in our lives is meant as a test to enable us to develop our character (see *The Path of the Just,* Ch.1). Illness can be the most difficult challenge a person will face. The more serious the illness, the more courage one needs to cope well.

Even a mild illness of relatively short duration has its challenges. We are either in physical distress or have the frustration of not being able to do all that we would want to do. All the more so are the challenges of a chronic illness or a life-threatening one. By viewing all forms of illness as our courage seminar, we will be building up our courage as we learn to handle the situation.

Even when someone is healthy, the way one views illness will be a major factor in how one copes in times of challenge. Some people are very nervous when they think of the possibility of becoming ill. This is especially so when one had a relative with a certain illness and witnessed the debilitating effects of that illness. Some people become obsessed with specific illnesses. Anything resembling the symptoms of the disease is a cause of intense anxiety. This can cause tremendous suffering even if one remains healthy and ultimately dies peacefully in old age.

A healthy person who views all types of illness as a courage seminar might prefer to skip this seminar, but will still be able to view the possibility of illness in a character-developing light.

Accepting the A-mighty's will and realizing that this, too, is for your benefit will enable you to grow spiritually the entire duration of an illness. Your prayers will be uttered with more fervor. Your sense of helplessness can be a source of true humility and awareness of your total dependence on the will of the A-mighty. Do not view illness as a time out from life, but as an essential part of it.

Read stories about people who coped well with illness. Everyone agrees that if one maintains hope and is able to experience laughter and joy, one will have a better quality of life. In some situations this can seem almost impossible. That is why it is important to find role models of people who had the inner strength and courage to maintain positive emotional states when they were ill.

My daughter's father-in-law, Rabbi Avraham Baharan, a brilliant educator, was in the late stages of bone cancer. He maintained courage and good cheer the entire time. During a visit, not too long before he died, I asked him, "How are things going?"

"Everything is going exactly according to plan," he replied.

Knowing that the courage seminar you are attending has a clear plan makes it easier to have the necessary courage.

*I used to dread being ill for even a brief time. I felt powerless and helpless. I felt that life was passing me by. When I was ill with flu, I was extremely impatient for it to be over, even though it wasn't serious and would pass quickly. I once felt tired and without energy for over a week. Each day I was hoping that the next day I would feel better. But I felt weaker and weaker. I was diagnosed with mononucleosis. "Oh, no," I said to myself, "I've heard of people being debilitated with this for months and months."*

*"This is your courage seminar," I was told. "You will have this condition for a while. It's your choice how you will experience it emotionally. You can be upset, frustrated, depressed, and miserable, if that is the way you choose to experience your condition. But by viewing it as your growth seminar, you will accept the A-mighty's will and will be developing the character traits of humility and courage. You can experience serenity and an inner happiness during the entire time. Just remembering that you're the one who chooses what the experience will be like will make it much easier for you."*

*It took longer than I had expected to overcome mononucleosis. I had a number of setbacks after I thought that I was well enough to resume normal life. Eventually I did recover completely. The advice that I received transformed what could have been a most miserable and depressing situation into one long vacation during which I developed both spiritually and emotionally.*

# 47.

# ILLNESS OF FAMILY MEMBERS

Anyone who has a family needs the courage to deal with illness. Parents need courage when their children become ill. Children of all ages need courage when their parents become ill. Husbands and wives need courage when their spouse becomes ill. In short, we all need courage when someone we love becomes ill, especially when we are dependent on that person.

The illness of a family member is also part of our courage seminar. This applies even to minor illnesses which disrupt our lives. All the more so when the illness is major.

Transform your worries about the health and welfare of your loved ones into courage. This applies to a young couple whose first child has medical problems. This applies to a teenager whose parent has a serious illness. This applies to a middle-aged person whose parent has Alzheimer's, Parkinson's, or any other mentally or physically debilitating condition. This applies to a grandparent whose married children or grandchildren have a life-threatening disease.

Some people who are able to cope well with their own challenges find it more difficult when someone they love is suffering. Your own courage can be a source of strength for the person who is ill, just as the courage of a person who is ill can be a source of strength for relatives.

Twenty-two years ago, when my mother called me to tell me that my father had cancer and was scheduled for surgery in a couple of days, I felt devastated. It was like a bomb hit me. My father wasn't young, but he wasn't elderly. He had lost his father when he was only 3 years old. There were many things he did in his life that took tremendous courage.

I remember the anxiety I felt when I traveled to Baltimore to visit him in the hospital.

"I am ready to die whenever Hashem wants me to," he calmly told me. "But we have an obligation to live as long as we can."

With peace of mind, he gave me a list of instructions which included where he wanted to be buried and what should be written on his tombstone. ("He merited to hear Torah from the mouth of the Chofetz Chaim in Radin.")

My father's courage was the greatest single lesson that I ever received on death and dying. It strengthened me both before and after his death.

*Before I became religious, I did a lot of things that took courage. I parachuted out of planes. I went mountain climbing. I went rafting in* turbulent waters. And I felt that I could do anything. But when my fourth child was just two weeks old, he developed a high fever. I was told to rush him to the hospital, where they had to diagnose what the exact problem was. They did everything they could to lower the fever. The entire time I was terrified. My imagination went wild and this added to my anxiety. But I needed to have courage. I felt strongly that my own emotional state would have an effect on my baby. I didn't want to panic in the baby's presence. I realized that cognitively he couldn't understand anything I said. But I knew that if I could maintain a calm state it would have a positive effect on the baby. Out of my love for my newborn baby, I had the courage to cope as well as I did. I prayed to Hashem and I am deeply grateful that my prayers were answered. The entire time I knew that one can never know how events will turn out and courage is necessary to cope with every eventuality.

# 48

# COURAGE TO SAY, "I DON'T KNOW"

Many people will perform mental gymnastics to avoid saying, "I don't know." Depending on the context of a situation, these three words can be very difficult to say.

Have you ever had the experience of asking someone for directions, and the person told you to go right or left, and it was the wrong way? Why does this happen so frequently? Because many people lack the courage to say, "I don't know."

A physician who lacks the courage to say, "I don't know," might cause serious harm or damage. Some will say, "It's nothing," but it turns out that there was a serious medical issue that was not diagnosed properly. Doctors and people in related fields should rather say, "To me it doesn't seem like anything." This could be a true statement. Adding the words, "To me," opens the door for the patient to consult someone else who might find something that this doctor missed.

There are two opposite situations when people find it easier to say that they do not know. One is when a person has hardly any knowledge at all about a subject, and does not claim to have that knowledge. Everyone would prefer to know answers to the questions he is asked, but since he knows that this entire topic is not his domain, he does not find it that difficult to say, "I don't know."

On the opposite extreme is one who is a major expert on a topic. He knows very much about it. Since he is so confident in his knowledge of this area, he does not feel diminished by acknowledging what he does not know.

Every time you do not know something that you are asked about, have the courage to say, "I don't know." View every time you repeat this three-word sentence as yet another time that you are increasing your level of courage. This way, instead of feeling embarrassed that you do not know, you will be able to focus on the fact that you are increasing your level of courage.

*When I was in high school, all the students greatly respected a certain teacher for his integrity. Whenever he was asked about something that he didn't know the exact answer to, he would say, "I don't know now. I will do research and will try to come back with the correct answer." In contrast there were teachers who tried to make us think that they knew more than they actually did. We realized the reality. If those teachers knew how we felt, they would have told us that they did not know when they did not. This would have gained them greater respect, not less.*

*I would always say that I didn't know something if I didn't. But I used to feel bad about it. I wished that I had a better memory than I did. I wished I would have had a greater amount of knowledge. When my children would ask me questions that I couldn't answer, I felt very uncomfortable about having to say, "I don't know." But I was told that I should view this as a way that I would be increasing my courage. Moreover, I was teaching my children an important lesson in honesty. I remember one time when another parent was visiting my home and heard me say, "I don't know." I felt great when that person commented, "When I say, 'I don't know,' my voice expresses my bad feelings that I don't know. I see that you say you don't know with the same confident tone as you use when you do know. I would like to learn from you.*

# 49

# COURAGE OF SILENCE

There are instances when it takes courage to remain silent. It would be easier to speak up, but the right thing to do is to be silent. You express courage with your silence. And this silence is yet another step in increasing your level of courage.

An authority figure wants you to tell him something negative about another person. Normally you would do what this person asks you to do. But in this instance there is no practical, constructive benefit to be gained from telling him the negative information. So you politely decline. If he persists, it is up to you to consistently refuse. Your silence is an expression of courage.

Someone is angry because an item belonging to him was broken. He asks, "Who did it?" You know who did it. The person is standing right next to you. You feel like saying, "He did it." But that person is not admitting he did it. For you to say, "He did it," would embarrass that person. You plan to speak to the guilty party in private and you know that you will be able to influence him to pay for what he broke. At this point it is difficult for you to remain silent since the person thinks that you might possibly be the one who did it. Since you are going to make certain that he gets payment for his loss, it is proper for you not to embarrass the person who lacks the courage to acknowledge his actions right away. Your silence is an act of courage.

You were invited to a wedding. Other acquaintances were not invited. Those people are talking about the wedding and you hear from the way they are speaking that they feel badly about not having been invited. You feel like boasting, "I was invited," but you remain silent. Saying that you were invited and plan to go would arouse their envy. Your silence is an expression of courage and self-mastery.

You did extremely well on a difficult test. Others did poorly. The fact that you do not tell them that you received a high grade is likely to make them assume that you did as poorly as they did. Your remaining silent and not telling them that you received a perfect score is an expression of courage.

Someone insults you. You can easily say something in return that would be the equivalent of a devastating knockout punch. You do not say a word. Your silence is an expression of courage.

*I read about people who were willing to undergo extreme torture not to reveal the identity of comrades in arms or the hiding place of Jews in World War II. This has always inspired me not to speak* lashon hara (*negative speech about others*) *even when it has been difficult to remain silent.*

*I run a company. I am what you would call a know-it-all controlling boss. My self-esteem is based on my being needed by everyone for my knowledge and know-how. I took an overseas vacation for a few weeks and the office ran quite well without me. When I returned, I decided to give everyone more freedom to do things on their own. They thrived. At the next general staff meeting, I asked everyone for their feedback about how things were going. The employees praised me for believing in them and not giving constant orders and suggestions. My silence had been extremely difficult for me. It took an act of courage for me to remain silent and realize that I'm not as indispensable as I had always assumed.*

# 50.

# COURAGE TO FACE ANGER

W hen people are angry with us, we find it distressful. The negative energy that is manifest in the tone of voice and words that are said in anger easily cause a person to react with tension and stress. Many react to anger with their own anger. Angry looks in someone's eyes or angry body language can be scary. It takes courage to face an angry person. Every time someone speaks to you angrily, you have yet another opportunity to build up your courage.

Some people are so frightened of the anger of others that it prevents them from speaking up for their rights. Others manipulate them by expressing anger. This is one of the factors that motivate people to get angry. They know that others will give in to them if they express anger. They know that even people who are not intimidated by mild anger will often give in when they are faced with rage or fury.

People who fear the anger of others often try to avoid this by not expressing their wants, wishes, needs, and opinions. They would rather do without than to assert themselves when they might be faced with anger.

View every encounter with an angry person as a way to upgrade your level of courage. Try to understand why the other person is angry with you. Perhaps he has a valid reason. Then have the courage to acknowledge the rightness of his basic position. Even though you would have preferred for him to speak to you in a calm manner, that does not negate the validity of his position. So deal with the factors that bother him and apologize or negotiate.

If you feel that a person who is angry with you does not have a valid reason for being angry, respectfully explain your position. Avoid saying anything that will provoke more anger. Do not insult that person or speak sarcastically. King Solomon gives us this formula for melting anger (*Proverbs* 15:1): "A soft reply subdues anger." Speak softy and gently, both with the content of your words and the tone of voice.

People who become angry easily usually have suffered a lot in their lives. View someone's anger as that person's pain. Have compassion for an angry person.

In my book *Anger: The inner teacher,* I have written about how to overcome your own anger. There you will find how to remain centered and balanced when dealing with the anger of others. Here we will mention two helpful techniques.

One, imagine that the person who is angry with you is a distant mountain. Listen to what he has to say. But see him as if he is far away.

Two, imagine that this person is on stage and you are up in the balcony watching yourself in the audience watching this person. This is known as double dissociation and makes you less vulnerable to the angry energy.

*Growing up I was always intimidated by the anger of others. I would avoid getting people angry. I would claim that this is because I love peace and don't want to cause a quarrel. But when I am totally honest with myself, I realize that I am afraid of the anger of others. I might say, "I'm not really afraid. But I don't like anger." The reality was that I am afraid. The proof is that if the person who gets angry has a soft or squeaky voice and doesn't look very strong, I can easily face his anger.*

*I was told to view the anger of others as my courage-building lessons. What I noticed right away was that I no longer avoided confrontations like I previously did. What was fascinating to me was that my assumptions that people would get angry was overly exaggerated. Not many people did actually get angry at me. And if they did, my reframe enabled me to look forward to the experiences. Not fearing anger allows me to try to get refunds, to not let a dishonest taxi driver cheat me, to express an unpopular opinion, to ask people for favors that I really need but would refrain from asking for them. All of these and many similar patterns were difficult for me when I feared anger. Overcoming fear of anger for me has served as an emotional firewalk.*

# 51.

# "SO WHAT IF THEY STARE?"

*"Stop being afraid of being stared at," I was told over and over again while I was growing up. "You're not a snowman and you won't melt."*

*This was a true statement. I was not a snowman and staring would not cause me loss, injury, or pain. Even so I was not able to overcome my extreme discomfort. I did everything I could to avoid the stares of others.*

Every time someone stares at you, you have yet another opportunity to increase your level of courage. Imagine how you would feel if the stares of others sent you courage-increasing rays. From now on that is one way you can perceive stares. You can use them as tools for increasing your feelings of empowerment.

Jewish law teaches that we should not stare at people who are eating. Staring at them as they eat is likely to cause them discomfort. But on the receiving end of a stare, you have the ability to utilize it as a tool for further empowerment.

The more comfortable one feels about oneself, the less being stared at will be considered a problem. In reality there is no practical difference if one walks down an empty street or a street full of staring people. We are not dealing with a situation that is dangerous. Those with vivid imaginations have the ability to imagine that the streets are full of people cheering and wishing one well. For those who might argue that this is not real, neither is being intimidated by being stared at. The main difference is that the cheering imagery is much more enjoyable than experiencing anxiety because of someone's stares.

I remember walking on Shabbos with my father to his synagogue in East Baltimore. The neighborhood was a tough one. There were not very many individuals with black hats and black suits. I would feel a bit uncomfortable. But my father kept telling me not to be self-conscious. He radiated self-confidence and friendliness. People of all races would ask him for his blessings and prayers. His good-naturedness enabled him to view everyone as a friend and people reciprocated.

*I was beginning to become Torah observant. I observed Shabbos and kept kosher. But I wouldn't wear a yarmulka on my head. I felt intimidated by the fear that people will stare at me.*

*A friend of mine who was newly observant approached me and said, "I realize that you are afraid of people staring at you. Let me tell you how I deal with this. I view every stare as a chance for me to make a statement. Whenever I can, I tell people that my hair covering serves as a reminder of the Creator above. I tell people how this gives me a sense of empowerment. This is a reminder to me that I am a child of the Creator. In practice I nod my head and send a friendly smile toward staring eyes. Many people nod and smile back. I have found my general level of courage growing greatly."*

*I limp. I realize that people tend to stare at anyone who looks a little different. I received my injury in a car accident. The car was totaled. I view the stares of others as reminders to be grateful that I am alive and have regained my ability to walk.*

# 52.

# COURAGE TO ASK FOR ADVICE

*I was doing poorly in school. I managed to just get by. My biggest problem was that I was finding it more difficult to read than did the other kids in the class. At my age, everyone thought it was obvious that I could read well, but I couldn't. I lacked the courage to approach anyone for help. I was afraid to admit that at my age I couldn't read well. Finally I had a teacher who recognized that I had this problem. The teacher suggested that I go to an expert in teaching reading. I did and it changed my entire life. I did so much better in school. I actually began to enjoy the reading which had previously been painful to me causing me to read as little as possible. I wish that I would have had the courage to ask for advice about my reading years before.*

*My spouse and I didn't communicate well. We argued over trivialities. We both would say, "We need to improve our communication." But we didn't have a clue about what we needed to do differently. We spoke about going for counseling. But neither of us were motivated enough to actually acknowledge that we needed someone to help us.*

*This lack of courage caused us tremendous misery for years. Only when the situation was totally unbearable did we consult someone. We both realized that if we would have had the courage to do this a long time ago, it would have prevented much suffering.*

*Fear held me back in so many ways that it would take a long time for me to describe them all. I thought that this was my nature and I couldn't do much about it. I also was too embarrassed to tell anyone else that I was such a coward. Deep down I always wished that I could speak to someone who would help me overcome my fears. I finally realized that I didn't need to say to anyone that I was cowardly. I needed to find someone or a few people to whom I could turn for advice on how to gain additional courage. This approach made the whole idea of asking for advice much easier for me. I asked someone, "You seem to me to have a lot of courage. Can I ask you a few questions about it?" The first time I did this it was very difficult for me. But just doing this once made it easier for me to ask for advice in other areas also especially as that first person's input about courage was helpful.*

We can all benefit from the advice of wise and experienced people. Besides gaining from their knowledge, you can gain from their objectivity.

We all have areas where we will not do as well as we possibly could. There will be people you can ask for advice on how to improve. Whatever skills you lack, there will be someone you can consult on how to gain those skills. Have the courage to seek them out.

Many students could gain a lot from asking for advice on how to concentrate better, how to remember better, how to read faster and with greater comprehension. Many parents could gain a lot by asking for advice on how to create a peaceful, harmonious home where they bring out the best in their children. Many teachers could gain from consulting master teachers with much experience. Many businessmen and professionals could gain from consulting experts in their field. Almost everyone could gain by consulting appropriate people about how to become a better person. Have the courage to ask for advice.

A person who is needlessly sad needs to learn the skill of happiness and joy. A person who becomes angry easily needs to learn the skill of maintaining calm in challenging situations. A person who suffers from worrying needs to learn the skill of mastery of one's thoughts. Most people need to learn to upgrade their ability to find positive reframes for situations and occurrences. Have the courage to consult knowledgeable people.

What if you consult one person and it proved not to be helpful? Have the courage to ask someone else. What if you have already consulted many people and nothing anyone said really helped you long term? Have the courage to approach still more people. Or have the courage to go back to one of those people to see if what they can tell you now will be more helpful than it was in the past. Have the courage to consult people about whom you should consult.

*I have always found it easy to consult people. My father had a great rabbi whom he would consult frequently. He would tell his children how fortunate he was that he was able to consult this giant of a teacher for many dilemmas. If there was an area where this rabbi felt that my father needed to consult someone with specific expertise, my father viewed consulting that person as an extension of asking his mentor. I learned from my father that it is wise to ask experts for advice. I was surprised when I found out that a lot of people were hesitant to do this. Of course, one needs to be selective about whom to ask. But the general idea of asking for advice seems to me to be a very valuable resource.*

# 53.

# COURAGE TO BEGIN AGAIN

It takes courage to begin again after the collapse of a project, an organization, or a business. One has spent considerable time and energy and things did not work out as well as one would have wished. Experiencing this makes one more wary about the future. The more "failures," the more courage that you need in order to begin again and the greater amount of courage that you gain when you do actually begin again.

In reality, each moment is an entirely new world. Every moment is a moment we should utilize in the best way possible. At the present time, whatever happened in the past is ancient history. Our task is to say and do what is the best and wisest thing right now.

Regardless of how many projects you already worked on that did not succeed, if you knew for certain that the next project would be an immense success, you would definitely do what you could to make it succeed. When you are increasing your courage, you are succeeding at building your character.

What some people might label "failure" is a success when you successfully grow from the experience.

One of the ultimate begin-again stories was Rabbi Akiva. He had twenty-four thousand students who died within a short period of time. He started over again with five students, who all became great Torah leaders. His courage is our role model.

*I strongly wanted to get married. I met many potential marriage partners, but it took a long time until I became engaged. Everyone wished me well with great joy. Finally, I, too, was going to be married. About three weeks before the wedding date, my fiancé had a change of heart. There weren't really serious complaints about me. But fear of making the commitment caused every minor foible of mine to be perceived as grave and serious faults. I had to begin the entire process all over again. This took a great amount of courage on my part. Fortunately, this courage has helped me in many ways. I became engaged about a half year after the broken engagement and I was totally dedicated to do all I could to create a harmonious marriage.*

*During the Holocaust I lost my entire family, my wife, children, my parents, my siblings, and the vast majority of my friends. Beginning again seemed at first like a superhuman feat. But day by day, I made the choices that I needed to make. The courage it took was such that I wouldn't believed that I possessed. But my belief in the A-mighty gave me the inner strength to survive and to rebuild.*

# 54.

# COURAGE TO QUIT A PROJECT

Persistence is a wonderful quality. Without persistence people give up too soon and fail to accomplish. But there comes a moment when we need to realize that it is time to quit the present project we are working on.

We might realize that we will never reach the goal we had set for ourselves. This can be a painful awareness. We might have invested a lot of time and energy into the project. Stopping now might retroactively make our efforts seem like a waste of time. We might have already invested hoards of money. We might feel that if we persist we still may turn a profit or at least get our money back. By stopping now, all that money will go down the drain. It takes courage to say to oneself, "It took me until now to realize that this won't work. It's wiser to stop right now than to keep wasting even more time and throwing good money after bad."

At times you might still consider it a realistic possibility that the project will work out. But it will be preferable and wiser to engage in something that has greater chances of success. It takes courage to quit what you are doing and to begin again utilizing a better alternative.

How do you know whether it is wiser to have the courage to continue persistently or to have the courage to quit now and start something else? There is no magic formula. But when you have the courage to make either choice, your decision will be based on the most intelligent move to make. Lack of courage might cause you to make the wrong choice out of fear.

"Quitters are losers!" This is frequently true, but not always. At times, quitters will be winners since they can then devote their time, money, and energy to a project that seems more likely to succeed. It would be a mistake to quit prematurely. Weigh the entire picture to figure out your best course of action. But do not let fear of quitting lead you in the wrong direction.

We are never guaranteed success with the choices we make. Let each decision you make increase your knowledge and wisdom. Your lifetime course of consistently gaining more wisdom has added yet another experience that will ultimately help you make wise decisions in the future.

*I was suffering greatly. My anxiety level was very high. I was a relatively young man and my business was tremendously successful. Together with my partners we seemed to have been making the right decisions time and time again. Then we hit a rough spot. The business was suffering unprecedented losses. My partners were panicking and we all were feeling tremendous tension from the stress we were experiencing. I tried to become calmer. I would repeat affirmations about being calm, but it didn't work. I tried to maintain serenity, but I just couldn't.*

*I remember how much better I felt when it was suggested to me to forget about being calm and serene. Rather, I should focus on gaining courage. It was unrealistic for me to become totally calm and at ease. What was realistic for me was to increase my level of courage. I found this empowering and it helped me clear my mind to think about the entire situation with greater clarity of thought. I realized that with a greater amount of courage, I could make a more objective decision about whether to continue or change what I was doing.*

# 55.

# COME TO THE RESCUE

King David (*Psalms* 34:14) gave us a prescription for long life: "Guard your tongue from evil and your lips from speaking deceit." The Chofetz Chaim (d. 1933), who spread the Torah principles of refraining from harmful speech and gossip, lived to the age of 94. There are many who seek to emulate this great sage by making an effort not to needlessly say anything negative about other people.

Unfortunately there are others who are not yet committed to refrain from negative speech. If you are in the presence of one of these people as they are maligning or slandering someone, come to the rescue. Have the courage to speak up in defense of the person being spoken against. This is not always easy. Build up the strength of character and courage to stop negative speech.

Do not be intimidated by someone who has a need to put others down. Be respectful of them, just as you want them to be respectful of you and the person they are speaking against. Having the courage to speak up makes you a hero. There are people who walk on hot coals to increase their sense of courage and inner strength. They do this to strengthen their fortitude. You can view your putting a halt to evil speech as your personal firewall. You become a positive force in a person's life when you protect him from being spoken against.

What if you respectfully and politely ask someone to stop speaking against others and he refuses to stop? "Who are you to tell me what to do?" he might say. Or, "I'll say whatever I feel like." Be persistent. Remain respectful and polite the entire time. Perhaps you can change the subject. The more subtly you do this, the better. Just start talking about something else that will capture his interest.

Whenever possible, try to judge the victim of the negative speech favorably. "Perhaps there are details omitted that change the entire picture," you can say. Or, "You can never know what is actually the total reality."

The stronger your commitment not to allow anyone to speak against others in your presence, the more successfully you will come up with creative ways and means to protect the dignity of another human being. One method is to begin coughing intensely as you would if something were totally disgusting and mention that you are allergic to negative speech and it is crucial to speak about something else.

*I used to be very careful not to speak negatively about other people. But I was shy and it was difficult for me to tell people to stop speak-*

*ing against others. At times I felt really awful about myself for not speaking up. But I was so intimidated by others that it was almost as if I lost my power of speech.*

*I witnessed someone tell a group of strangers, "Please don't talk against him because he's a human being and so am I. I would greatly appreciate your changing the topic."*

*I was highly impressed with his courage and I told him so.*

*"It's not really courage," he said. "No one has ever hit me for asking them to change the subject. I'm doing a favor to the person spoken about, and also for the speaker. He is spiritually better off by not maligning another person. Even if someone doesn't realize this benefit, I realize it. This makes it relatively easy for me. When you try this yourself, you'll see that it's easier than you thought." He was right.*

*I always felt that I should ask people to stop speaking against others when they tried to do so in my presence. I found this extremely hard to do. I feared that they would become angry with me. I once witnessed someone stop others from speaking negative gossip by asking them, "If someone would be speaking against you, would you want me to stop them?" They nodded their heads, "Yes," and got the message. This seemed to me to be easier than what I had tried earlier. After using this pattern a few times, I found it easy to do. Basically I was telling them that the same way I was defending the victim of their speech I would be committed to defend them if it were ever necessary.*

# 56.

# INSULTS

The power of an insult is up to you, the receiver of the insult. No one likes to be insulted. The Torah prohibits us from insulting other people and in my book *Power of Words,* I have elaborated on this topic. Nevertheless, the level of distress we will experience, or even whether we will experience distress, will depend on how we subjectively reframe the insult.

When you evaluate an insult as awful, terrible, or horrible, you will suffer from the words that the insulter has sent your way. By reframing an insult negatively, you needlessly give others power over you. If you find a positive way to view an insult, you will be saved from much suffering.

In my book *Happiness: Formulas, Stories, and Insights* (pp.182-4), a number of ideas are mentioned how to render insults less painful or harmless. From the perspective of courage, we can view each insult as yet another opportunity to increase our level of courage.

If someone were to offer you a considerable amount of money for each insult thrown your way, if the amount were large enough you would react with happiness or joy to all insults. The distress would last for only a few seconds. The benefits would last a long time. When you increase your level of courage, you will be gaining immensely your entire life.

Fear of insults can cause people much suffering. When you view each insult as a booster shot that is increasing your courage, insults will actually empower you.

You might practice this exercise: As you walk down the street, imagine that every individual is throwing insults at you (just with their words). Visualize yourself feeling an inner courage, an inner strength, an inner dignity. The more negative others are, the more courage you are gaining. You can even say to yourself, "The more negative they are, the more inner resources I am building up in my brain. My courage is getting stronger and stronger."

When you totally master this, you will actually feel positive when someone insults you. As Maimonides (Commentary to *Ethics of the Fathers* 4:4) related: There was a righteous person who was asked, "What was the most joyous day of your life?" He replied that it was a day when he was on a ship. Other passengers mocked and jeered him and threw garbage on him.

This was a day of liberation for that person. He now realized that he had such a strong self-image and so much courage that nothing anyone said could make him feel bad. So instead of feeling pain about the incident, he viewed it as the happiest day of his life. He was now free from all concerns about whether people would praise or insult him. As you mentally visualize yourself being able to do this, you will be increasing your sense of freedom from the negativity of others.

*Insults used to cause me a tremendous amount of pain. But I worked on myself daily to have enough courage to melt any insults that came my way. If someone were angry at me for a valid reason, I would take heed of the underlying message and do what I could to improve myself and improve my relationship with this person. But if there was nothing I could do, I would say to myself, "This, too, is increasing my courage." I don't fear any insults that I might hear in the future, because I say to myself, "If anyone tries to say something insulting to me, I will utilize what he says to increase my courage."*

*A major benefit that I gained from this is that I used to be overly concerned with the questions, "What will people say about me?" And, "What will people think?" Now that I'm not worried about insults, these questions no longer bother me like they once did.*

*Insults would overwhelm me. If someone insulted me, I used to become totally obsessed with what that person said. In my brain I would repeat the insult over and over again, each time feeling highly distressed. It was suggested that I look in a mirror and visualize myself having intense courage. After I felt this courage, I would repeat, "The words of anyone else can have power over me only if I allow them to. Nothing anyone says to me can take away my intrinsic value of being a child of the Creator." I used my ability to repeat things over and over again to repeat empowering messages.*

# 57.

# SAVING TIME THROUGH COURAGE

ourage can be a great time-saver. There are instances when you find yourself in a situation that is eating up a lot of your precious time. You would like to say or do something about it, but you find it difficult to do so. Utilize these situations as yet more opportunities to build up your courage.

*I am friendly and like talking to people. Many of the people I talk to are lonely and need a listening ear. I realize that I am doing an act of kindness by listening. Nevertheless, when I was busy I really needed to end the conversation. But I didn't have the heart to do so. I was afraid that the people who were talking to me would be upset with me if I ended the conversation before they were finished. I read about assertiveness and realized that this is the quality that I needed. The first few times I tried to be assertive I abruptly said, "Sorry, I have to go now." The speed at which I ended the conversation was distressful to the people I spoke to. Someone pointed out to me that I was too abrupt. The reason I was abrupt was because it was so difficult for me to say that I had to leave.*

I practiced ending conversations smoothly. I would say things like, "It was enjoyable talking to you. To be continued at a different time."

Now that I knew that I could end a conversation when I felt it was time to end it, I felt more comfortable the entire time. Every time I end a conversation, I say to myself, "This is another act of courage for me." Many people wouldn't consider this as courage since they do this so easily. But since this had been difficult for me, it was a courage builder.

When people used to invite me for various occasions, I used to feel obligated to go whether or not I wanted to and whether or not the person really needed me to be there. Now that I view turning down an invitation as an act of courage, I weigh situations more objectively. When I feel a true obligation to go or when I feel that my going would be greatly appreciated, I accept invitations. But since I have the courage to say yes or no, I view my going any place as my decision and choice. I no longer go places and then feel resentful that I am spending time at events where my presence is not necessary.

When I am at a meeting or a lecture, I find it very difficult to leave before it is over. At times leaving in the middle would be disruptive or would make someone feel bad. Then I make a supreme effort to stay even when I would prefer to leave. But I have worked on my courage level to know that I can leave whenever I feel it is appropriate for me to do so. In the beginning I started building up this courage by walking out for a minute or two and returning. Once I saw that I could get up and leave, I made choices about whether to stay or not based on the total picture of my life that day, rather than feeling trapped out of fear. If the speaker would take offense or feel hurt, I view my staying as an act of kindness. It comes from a conscious decision that I am glad to make.

I am a kind person and love doing things for people. But at times people ask me if I could do things that would take me a lot more time and energy that I am really able to spend. When I was younger I would take on more projects than I could handle. I still wish that I could do more acts of kindness for others, but I need to ration my limited amounts of time wisely. I apologize profusely when I feel unable to spend time on something. I view these incidents as courage building. I used to feel guilty even when I knew rationally that it was impossible for me to do everything. Now I have a more balanced perspective.

# 58

# THE COURAGE TO OFFER HELP

When you offer to help someone, most people are appreciative. They benefit greatly not only by the actual help, but also because of the knowledge that there are kind people who are willing to volunteer to help them. But some people react negatively when others offer their help. After a number of these experiences, it might take courage to keep offering help to people since you are aware of the possibility that their response could be irritating.

I recently met someone who told me about his relative who works eight hours a day on major deals. During an entire year only about two or three deals actually go through. He gains enough financially from these deals that he is able to live comfortably. The rest of the deals he tries do not come to fruition. Would it not make more sense to just try for the deals that do go through and not waste time on the ones that do not? The answer is, "Yes." But without the gift of prophecy it is not possible to know in advance just which deals will be successful. All the other attempts are the background that make the successful deals possible.

The same applies to offering to help people. It is worth making hundreds of offers a year if only two or three will be accepted. The value of kindness cannot be measured with money. The reality is that many people will be grateful for your offer to help and will accept your help rather than just two or three a year. In case someone does react with irritation, this too will enable you to upgrade your level of courage. If every person you offered to help would appreciate it and be grateful, you would not be building up your level of courage.

*I was on a city bus and a little boy about the age of 3 got on the bus with his mother. The little boy walked ahead of his mother and tried to climb on a seat all by himself. Since the bus was beginning to start moving, I reached out to help the little boy climb on the seat.*

*"Do you want my boy not to learn how to climb on a seat by himself?" she irrationally yelled at me. "If people like you keep trying to do things for him instead of letting him do them himself, he will be highly limited."*

*I didn't exactly enjoy this tongue-lashing on a bus full of people. But I have to admit that if such a situation arises again, I am still committed to help a young child get on his seat before the bus starts moving.*

*In an office, I saw someone who was having trouble working a certain computer program. I was highly experienced with that program and offered assistance.*

*"Don't you think that I am competent and could do this myself?" was the annoyed response.*

*To me if someone offers to help me learn something, it doesn't mean that the person thinks I'm incompetent. But if this person feels that way, I need to respect his feelings. Nevertheless, I am committed to offer assistance when I feel that someone needs it. Unless someone tells me otherwise, I will assume that they would appreciate the help.*

*I tend to notice when people lose their tempers easily. I, too, used to have a bad temper. I worked long and hard on mastering the ability not to get angry in the first place and if I did become angry, to express myself in a relatively calm way. I would like others to gain from my experience. I have found that some people are open to listen to what I have to say. Others tell me, "I can handle my anger myself," even though the way they say this to me shows me they can't. Yet others, respond in an angry tone of voice, "I don't have a problem with my temper. If others would just behave properly, I wouldn't get angry."*

*Before I offer suggestions to people with anger issues, I realize that this trait of theirs might lead to their becoming angry with me for offering to help. But if I am able to help only a few people, I feel it's worth the price of facing angry reactions. This helps me become a more courageous person.*

# 59.

# COURAGE TO FACE THE UNKNOWN

e all need to deal with the unknown. It is just a matter of degree. When we wake up in the morning, it's impossible to know how the day will turn out.

When we need to make a major decision, the outcome of our various options are always unknown. That is why important decisions can be so difficult. Even if we do a lot of research and we weigh every piece of data carefully, we can never know how our lives will turn out with each option.

People who are forced by circumstances to move to a different country are facing the unknown. The fewer resources of money, friends, and relatives that one has, the more difficult the change may be.

You can view making major moves as a courage-developing seminar. This applies when you change schools, change jobs, move to a new location, and everything similar.

*As a child I was fascinated to read stories about people who traveled to faraway places. Some did so to seek wealth, or at least to make a decent living. Others did so out of a sense of adventure. They were pioneers and explorers who willingly chose to travel to seek fame, fortune, or just plain excitement. Yet others were exiled from their land because of prejudice and persecution. A common theme is that when they started on their journey, they knew there were many risks and they had no guarantee as to how things would turn out in the end.*

*When I lost my job after many years, I felt overwhelmed. I was a bit old to look for a new job. But I was determined that I was going to do something meaningful with my life. My situation wasn't as dramatic as many of the stories that I had read. But there was a common factor: I needed courage to stay in good spirits and to optimistically look for opportunities. I had my health, and I did have much more life experience than those just starting out. I was committed to view my situation as one that would build my courage. This helped me cope with one of the most difficult time periods in my entire life.*

*I had relatives who hid in forests during World War II. Other relatives of mine emigrated to foreign countries where they didn't know anyone and they didn't speak the language. And yet others were exiled to the harsh climate of Siberia. After the war, when I met these people, I was extremely impressed with the courage they had gained from their ordeals. Whenever anything was difficult in my life, I would tell myself, "Your situation is much lighter than the conditions of your relatives. Their courage helped sustain them. Now their courage will serve as my role model." These thoughts empowered me and kept me going when I felt discouraged.*

# 60.
# QUOTES

There is a helpful tool known as, "Using quotes." This tool is useful for situations when you would like to say something but don't yet have the courage to say it directly. While you are working on upgrading your level of courage, using quotes can help you, as it were, test the waters. You can say almost anything you wish with quotes. Therefore this tool needs to be handled with care.

Here are some examples:

- "I've heard some people say that…"
- "There are people who think that…"
- "I would find it difficult to say this myself. But I've read that…"
- "I've read an editorial that… Would you agree?"
- "I've read that almost everyone would benefit by increasing their level of courage. Is there some way that you personally think you could benefit?"

All tools can be used beneficially or harmfully. Take a hammer, for instance. A hammer can be used to build and it can be used to break and destroy. Similarly, with quotes you can say things to someone that otherwise you would find too distressful to say. Use quotes to help others. Utilize quotes to praise and give positive feedback when you find it difficult to say them directly or you feel that the person you are telling them to would feel awkward. For example, "I've heard people say that you are doing a wonderful job." Utilize quotes to stop people from harming themselves. Utilize quotes to motivate and inspire positive behavior. Refrain from using quotes to insult someone in ways that you would not be able to do directly.

When you see that someone else has the same issues as you do in some area, you can say, "I had the same issue myself, and I was told…" This way you are merely reporting what was said to you.

Some people even quote themselves. They say things like, "I once told someone, 'It's not wise to do things that are harmful to your health.' How would you feel if someone said that to you?" When people tell you that they view it as an act of caring, you can feel free to encourage them.

*I was shy and timid. There were many things that I would like to say to others, but I felt intimidated to say them. Someone suggested to me that I use "quotes." For example, I would like to stop people from speaking negatively against others. But I find this difficult. I was* advised to try saying, "I heard that people who speak against others usually focus on the faults they themselves have. Don't you find this statement fascinating?"

I needed to increase my level of courage to say this. When I actually did, it was so much easier than I would have imagined.

I observed an elderly man tell a child who was doing something dangerous, "When I was your age, my mother told me not to do things in this way. My mother loved me and didn't want me to get hurt. I suggest that you listen to my mother's advice." To me it was humorous to hear someone close to 80 years old quote his mother like this. But it worked. The child stopped doing the dangerous thing and he accepted it in good spirits.

When I see people raising their voice in anger at someone to get their way, I frequently tell them, "I have a friend named Bob Burg who wrote a book entitled, 'Winning Without Intimidation.' He has done considerable research and has found that you will be more successful in getting someone to listen to what you have to say when you speak in a friendly tone of voice. Major companies hire him to train their employees. Why not try a friendly approach and see if this works for you!"

# 61.

# FOCUS ON THE BENEFITS

A major factor why some people feel intimidated when they try to influence or persuade others is because they have not been successful in the art of persuasion. The more skillful someone is in this area, the more positive he will feel about trying. While there are many principles and tools for persuasion, there is one key factor that can make a major difference.

When you try to influence someone to buy a product or service that he will benefit from, focus on the benefits he will gain. When you try to influence someone to take any action such as attend a lecture, read a book, or go someplace, clarify what the benefits will be to this person. If you are trying to influence someone to donate money to charity or to a worthy cause, focus on how this person gains eternally and how this will benefit the people who are being helped.

A major principle in focusing on the benefits are: What benefits are valued by this specific person? Some people focus on the benefits that would motivate them. They are unsuccessful when they try to motivate others because they do not take that individual's personal criteria into consideration. Ask people: "What is important to you? What motivates you to do the things that you do?"

People who find it difficult to influence others are focusing on their own feelings of discomfort. When you focus on the benefits that the person you influenced will gain, you will find it easier. You know that what you are trying to influence this person to do will be beneficial for him. Your idealism will make it much easier for you to speak up. View what you say to influence someone to buy, to donate, to improve, to stop doing something that is self-destructive or self-sabotaging as an act of kindness. When you convey your inner awareness to the other person, you will have a greater chance of being successful.

When you know for certain that someone will be grateful to you for what you are telling him, you would be glad to speak up. The difficulty is when at present the person might resent what you are saying or might become angry with you. As you focus on the benefits, you will be able to transcend the initial discomfort on your part. Perhaps in the end he will be grateful and perhaps not. But either way you know that what you are doing for this person is for his benefit. Even if you personally will also gain, let his benefits be uppermost in your mind.

*I knew someone who frequently lost his temper. I had often thought of suggesting that he do something about it. I would have liked to have* told him to read a book on the topic or to speak to a counselor. But I was afraid to make any suggestions. I was afraid that he will scream at me and tell me that he doesn't get angry. My own fears outweighed my concern for his loss resulting from his anger.

Eventually I saw that he was much calmer than before. Even in anger-provoking situations he spoke respectfully. I was curious about what helped him make the change. I waited for an opportune time. He was telling a few people how he had made an effort to change and how he has made much progress.

I asked him, "What motivated you to work on overcoming anger?"

"I met someone who saw me blow up," he told me. "I hadn't known this person for very long. But he had the courage to suggest that I work on my anger. The way he said it, I saw that he sincerely cared about my welfare. I will be forever grateful to him."

I am a salesman. The last ten years I have been much more successful than I was the first twenty years that I was in the field. What was the difference? I personally felt very positive about the items I sold. I naturally thought that others would be influenced to purchase what I was selling when I told them what I liked about each item. Then I became aware of the effectiveness in finding the specific benefits that each individual wants, needs, and appreciates. I was much more successful in a fraction of the time. When I couldn't meet the benefits of what someone wanted, I told him so. My sense of confidence has risen greatly because now I know that I am meeting the personal needs of my customers.

# 62.

# ONE HUNDRED YEARS FROM NOW

At times we give too much importance to a specific difficulty or the words of another person. This is especially so when we are not actually experiencing the difficulty. We are afraid that one day we will. We are not certain what someone will say to us, but we are afraid that what will be said will be painful and we do what we can to avoid the situation.

One tool for gaining a better perspective on our fears is to ask ourselves, "How will I look at this one hundred years from now?" It is unlikely that we will be alive one hundred years from now. And that is exactly what enables this perspective to give us a greater level of objectivity.

Someone might want to do a good deed, but is afraid that others might laugh at him. I suggest that he consider the following: A hundred years from now, how will the good deed be viewed and how will their laughing appear?

Someone might want to speak up and say what needs to be said. But he is afraid that others will be critical of what he said.

One hundred years from now, would it be better to have said what one wanted to say or would it have been better to remain silent?

Having a more comprehensive look at life and its true meaning will eliminate many needless fears and worries. This automatically gives us more courage. A tool that is helpful for this is to keep asking ourselves, "How will this be viewed one hundred years from now?"

Some people find it more helpful to ask themselves, "How will I view this in a year from now?" Or, "How will I view this ten years from now?" Since these are shorter amounts of time, they can relate to this better than one hundred years from now.

*I am terrified about making mistakes. This prevents me from trying many things. My fear is partly that I will feel bad about the mistakes because they will lower my self-esteem and partly because I am worried about what others will think of me. It was suggested that I ask myself, "What will the view of this mistake be in one hundred years from now?" This often makes me smile.*

*"How many mistakes of others that have been made one hundred years ago am I familiar with?" I ask myself. Not very many. One hundred years from now, how many people will care about my mistakes? While I still do all that I can to prevent mistakes, this makes me more objective about their importance. I feel calmer and ironically I do better than I would have if I were preoccupied with making mistakes.*

# 63.

# COURAGE AND SENSITIVITY

C ourage enables a person to say what is on his mind. This is wonderful for someone who has deep respect for other people. He realizes that each person is created in the image of the Creator and therefore he has a basic respect for every person he encounters. This is wonderful for someone who consistently sees the good in others, and even though he is aware of faults and limitations, he focuses on the good and the potential good. This is wonderful for someone who is on a lofty level and is full of love for other people and therefore would never want to needlessly cause anyone pain.

For courage to be valuable the owner of that attribute needs to be sensitive to the feelings of others. While he has the assertiveness to say whatever he feels like saying, he would not feel like saying something that is needlessly painful. He will be careful how he says whatever he says. He pays attention to the outcome of his messages. Since there are always a multitude of ways that any message can be worded, he will choose the most sensitive approach.

The biggest challenges come when one is angry. When we are angry with someone, we think negatively about that person. The more love and respect you have for people in general, the greater chance that even though you are angry you will still edit what you say. You will communicate your displeasure but in the best possible way for the specific situation.

If you think that because of your anger, you might speak harshly, wait until you calm down. When you are calm, you will think more clearly. Issues that seemed major at first might now appear to be quite trivial. You still might feel a need to say something about it, but your tone of voice and the content of what you say will be much more pleasant than if you spoke in the midst of your fury or rage.

There are those who have the assertiveness to speak up to some people but not to others. For example, there are individuals who are polite and respectful when talking to strangers. Even when they are angry with strangers, they are intimidated enough that they will not say anything insulting. But when they are angry with a member of their own family, they would say things they would never say to anyone else. Those who see this pattern in themselves (or it is pointed out to them by others) should make it a high priority to increase their sensitivity toward members of their family. Besides the intrinsic importance of not causing family members pain with words, it will then be safe for them to increase their ability to be assertive with more and more people. They will consistently speak with sensitivity.

*I remember meeting someone who was highly assertive. He was a very difficult person to get along with. He was the epitome of criticalness. If there was something that could possibly be seen as wrong, he would find it and focus on it. That alone was bad enough. But he felt that it was his duty to consistently point out to others what he found wrong with them or with what they said or did. The way he spoke didn't sound like it was coming from a sincerely caring place. He would boast that he had the courage to say anything to anyone. While he could have been a force for good, he caused many people distress and anguish. I used to associate assertiveness with this person and viewed it as a negative trait. I now realize that it's not assertiveness that was the problem, it's the way that he said things. At the time I was afraid to speak up to him. I felt that he wouldn't listen to me anyway. And if I were to suggest that he be more careful utilizing his power of words, he would insult me and put me down. Now I've developed enough courage that I could tell him that he's wrong for speaking as he does and that he needs to realize the amount of pain that he causes. Unfortunately, he died with this pattern. My lost opportunity to influence him to change has motivated me to be aware of this pattern in others and to speak up before it's too late.*

*I knew a kind, elderly scholar who could say anything to anyone. How fortunate for all the many people he influenced through his gentle approach to change. Out of his genuine profound love and concern for the welfare of others, he would point out ways that they could improve. Everyone he spoke to felt his deep respect for them and was grateful for the sensitive way he would point things out. He could say things that most people would shy away from. Because of his sensitive nature, the way he worded things and his kind tone of voice, his criticisms were greatly appreciated. They weren't even considered criticism. What he said was considered like a parent's suggestion on how to improve one's life.*

# 64.

# STUPIDITY IS NOT COURAGE

Courage is only courage when it is connected to wisdom. It is immature to risk one's life or health for fun or thrills. Not only is this immature, it is dumb. The Sages ask: "Who is a wise person?" And they answer: "One who sees the outcome" (*Tamid* 32a).

Driving a car at speeds high above the speed limit because one enjoys the feeling is stupid. Climbing in dangerous places when one does not have a valid need is not courage, but foolhardy. Walking in dangerous places just to prove to others that one is brave is reckless. Smoking cigarettes and feeling brave for doing so is a mistake that could one day prove fatal. Life is too precious to waste it with illusory courage.

To a lesser degree, to angrily tell a boss what you think of him when you are upset is not thinking ahead. One could lose one's job and find it difficult to get other jobs because of the outburst. If you want to give constructive criticism, do so with respect. Wait till you calm down and weigh what you say carefully. It is not courage to speak in a counterproductive way when you have the option of speaking in a way that might even be appreciated, at least tolerated. At times it can take a great degree of self-mastery and self-discipline not to say something that you intensely would like to say. But that is true courage.

If a person lacks the ability to have a comprehensive picture of the outcome of what he says or does, he would be much better off being a coward than being fearless. Fear saves lives. Fear protects us. The only problem is that we can have fear when it is not necessary or appropriate.

How can you judge whether a certain action is an act of courage or is just foolish daring? One criterion would be: If someone else did this, would you increase your respect for him or would you feel that he was doing something stupid? Another criteria would be: When I look back in my old age, will I be proud of what I did? And a more objective criteria would be: How would this be viewed by a wise and experienced elderly scholar? Would he advise me to do it? Or would he tell me to have the strength of character not to do it even though I felt like doing it?

*"Someone has to tell him what he needs to hear." The person who said this told him, considering what he did an act of courage. He did not accomplish anything other than getting himself fired from a job which he will find hard to replace.*

*When I visited my uncle in the intensive care ward of the hospital, the man in the next bed was unconscious. When his mother visited him, she told our family, "I told him again and again never to ride his motorcycle without a helmet. He felt that he was brave by not wearing his helmet. Now the doctor's don't give him very high chances of regaining consciousness. My older son was killed in a motorcycle accident, and I kept telling this son not to take stupid risks. But he refused to pay attention to what I told him."*

*When I was a child, we played a game that was a form of Russian roulette on a busy street. As a car was coming we would take turns running across the street. The one who was closest to a car was the winner. When a couple of children were seriously injured, the police made certain that we wouldn't continue playing this game. As an adult, I realize how stupid it was. I know now how I would feel if one of my children were to engage in this outrageous activity that should not be called a game.*

# 65.

# COURAGE VERSUS CHUTZPAH

hutzpah and courage have certain elements in common. But they are on the opposite end of the scale. Courage is a great virtue, while chutzpah is generally a negative trait.

An extreme definition of chutzpah has been given as someone who murders his parents and then claims that the court should be lenient with him because he is an orphan. A more common form is when a child speaks rudely to a parent, or when a student speaks to a teacher without respect. Chutzpah usually denotes that someone is doing or saying something that is not appropriate to do or say.

The sage Yehudah, the son of Teima, made two statements which are cited in the fifth chapter of *Ethics of the Fathers*. One is that we should, "Be as bold (*az*) as a leopard, light as an eagle, swift as a deer, and strong as a lion, to do the will of our Heavenly Father (ibid. 5:23)." Here we see that being bold is a virtue. In his next statement he uses the strongest language to condemn someone who is an *az ponim,* that is, someone who is brazen. What makes the difference between the quality that is very positive and the one that is very negative?

Here we will mention two distinctions. The praiseworthy quality is when someone is bold in order to fulfill the will of the Creator. This is the boldness of the courageous souls who withstood the Inquisition and adhered to the Torah even though they were risking their lives. This was the boldness of those who did what they could in the ghettos and concentration camps during the Holocaust to observe any possible *mitzvah.* This is the boldness of those who studied Torah when it was legally banned in the former Soviet Union. This is the boldness of those who observed *Shabbos* in the United States during the Great Depression in 1929 and the early '30's. This is the boldness that many people express in less dramatic situations when they observe Torah even though they are met with opposition.

Another distinction is that which is stated by Rabbi Chaim of Volozhin in *Ruach Chaim.* True courage is that which is inside your heart. You speak and act with courage, but you do not make an issue of it to anyone else. The Hebrew words for the negative form of brazenness is *az ponim*; this would be translated as, "Insolence on one's face." Here the chutzpah is recognizable on one's face. That is not the positive attribute of having inner courage.

If a person does have the negative trait of chutzpah, instead of trying to become meek and quiet, he should find positive ways to speak and act with courage. As the Vilna Gaon (*Commentary to Proverbs* 22:6) points out, we might not be able to change our temperament, but we can channel it in the proper direction. The more chutzpah one previously had, the more good he can now do. He will be able to do things that others would be afraid to do.

*When I was a young child, I was fearless around other people. I had the ability to say whatever came to my mind. At first I was too young to understand that I needed to be diplomatic about what I would say and how I said it. My parents kept telling me to refrain from saying things that they told me were chutzpadik to say. But I would argue, "Why is this chutzpah? This is the truth." I didn't realize that even with the truth, there are acceptable ways to speak and there are unacceptable ways. Teachers kept telling me that I have chutzpah and I would disagree with them. I didn't understand why they didn't understand that I was saying the truth. Finally I had a teacher who understood me. This teacher realized that I didn't mean to do anything wrong.*

*"You have a tremendous talent," my teacher told me. "You have a responsibility to use it for the good. You need to be more aware how the way you say things affect the people to whom you say them. You will be able to do many acts of kindness with your ability to say whatever you feel is right to say. You will be able to ask people to donate money to charity and worthwhile organizations. You will be able to suggest to people that they need to correct their actions and their traits.*

*But what you have is like explosives. They can be used for building and they can be used for destroying. The more powerful the explosives, the more careful one needs to be with them."*

*This teacher gave me a number of private lessons to help me differentiate between positive and negative ways to say things. This was the most important lesson in the world for me. I am very grateful that this teacher didn't just tell me that I had chutzpah. Rather this teacher showed me how to utilize it properly.*

## 66.

# DO NOT DENY POSSIBILITIES

Mentally prepare yourself to handle difficulties and challenges. This makes them easier to cope with. This also applies to disasters and catastrophes. There is a shock element when something happens that one did not expect would ever happen. As people often say, "I never imagined that this would happen to me."

Mentally preparing yourself is the positive polar side of worry. With worry one imagines something going wrong, and then feels anxiety about it in the present. Even if nothing ever goes wrong, one will have paid the price in emotional distress.

When you mentally prepare yourself, you imagine potentially distressful situations, and then you picture yourself handling them with courage. You see yourself accepting the will of the Creator. At the same time, you think of practical ways to solve the situation or at least deal with it in the wisest manner. As you think about future events, you are building your character, your spirituality, your ability to cope, and your courage.

Some people are so afraid of challenges that they deny the possibility of them ever occurring. They dread hearing people talking about accidents, illnesses, and other forms of painful events and suffering. They would be wise in building up their ability to cope. These are opportunities to increase one's love for the Creator. This love creates a magnificent state and creates true inner courage.

This love for the A-mighty is not all or nothing. It is not that either one has it or does not. Rather, like all traits, we have different measures of it. Even a small amount of this trait is extremely precious and valuable. The more you increase your love for our Father, our King, the greater your ability to live a joyous and meaningful life. Regardless of the situation, you will find meaning in it as you continually grow from all challenges. By repeatedly making mental pictures of having courage based on your love for the Creator, you will increase the power of both qualities.

*My house burned down. Two members of my family were seriously injured. They recovered, but it took a while. I was in shock for a long time. Since then I have met other people who have experienced similar traumatic events. I have seen people who have coped better and people who have coped worse. What was a key distinction? Those who realized that as humans we are always vulnerable and who mentally built up their courage to handle life's challenges were able to handle this the best. Those who felt that nothing like this would ever happen to them had their entire concept of their invincibility shaken to the core. I was somewhere in the middle. This taught me to make it a high priority to mentally visualize myself coping with courage in all eventualities.*

*My business went bankrupt and I found it painful. But I grew up in a home where my parents would repeat, "Everything that happens is part of the A-mighty's plans for us." They said this when things were going well and they said this when things were rough. They said this about illness and they said this about financial setbacks. They would tell their children, "We can never know what will happen in our lives. But we can know that if the Creator wants us to experience this then it is what we need to accept with trust in Him." Facing this major challenge which turned my life over, I learned to have a greater appreciation for that which they had taught me. Even when my business prospered I realized that this prosperity will last only as long as the A-mighty planned for it to do so.*

# 67

# COUNTERFEIT COURAGE

Counterfeit money is not real. Neither is counterfeit courage. Exaggerating the brave and heroic acts one has done to try to prove to other people that one has courage is a sign of a lack of courage. All the more so if someone were to fabricate an entire incident.

Ask yourself: Is there any way that I try to give others the impression that I have more courage than I really do? If the answer is, "Yes," look at this as feedback that you have a need to increase genuine courage.

A bank robber might view himself as having courage. After all, the dangers he faces are real. He could be arrested. He could be shot. He could be injured in a high-speed chase when he attempts to leave the scene of his crime. But his criminal act shows a lack of moral and ethical strength. While he is expressing a defiance for danger, what he has done cannot be deemed courage.

True courage for a bank robber would be to make amends

for the wrongs he has done even if he does not get caught. He can channel his propensity to do daring acts into constructive behavior. The question he should ask himself is, "What is the good I can do in the world now that I see that I am able to face danger?" Most people are not bank robbers. But many people can benefit by upgrading what they choose to do with their ability to face danger. The question for anyone who experienced facing danger with courage is, "What are the positive things that I can now do that I didn't previously think I could?"

If a person does a courageous act just in order to be able to boast about it, that, too, is counterfeit courage. When a person has true courage, he will not feel a need to boast. Boasting about courage is a sign of a lack of courage. Boasting is an expression that one needs the approval of others to feel good about himself. At times it can be appropriate to tell others about your courage to motivate and inspire them to develop their courage. At times people feel a need to tell others about their courage because this was not how they viewed themselves and now they need to integrate this awareness. The feedback of others is part of their process of integrating courage and making it more real.

*I have a serious handicap and I'm not able to do all the things that many people are able to do. I find it especially frustrating when I hear healthy people boasting about their feats of courage. I remember an* especially painful experience of hearing a group of people trying to outdo one another with their war stories. Some were actual war stories and some were about exciting adventures, such as mountain climbing, skiing, swimming in rough water, and traveling through a wild jungle. This made me feel inferior and caused me to become depressed.

An older man, who knew me well, saw the look on my face and privately asked me, "What's bothering you?" I felt embarrassed to tell him, but I knew that it would be helpful to share my feelings.

I told him how inferior I felt to these able-bodied people. He smiled at me and almost laughed. "Don't you realize that you have more real courage than these people do?" he said in a kindly manner. "They are boasting and some of them are exaggerating to such an extent that one would hardly consider what they said to be the truth. You have real courage. Day in and day out, you behave magnificently despite your handicap. If a prize for true courage would be given out, you would be the one to win it and not them."

To say that this gave me a boost would be a gross understatement.

# 68.

# "I DARE YOU"

§ ome people who feel a strong need to appear brave can be extremely vulnerable to dares. As soon as someone says to them, "I dare you to…" they immediately feel that they must do it. Do not allow yourself to fall into that trap. Even if the matter is minor and trivial, it is a dangerous start.

There are people who have been killed because of dares. "I dare you to drive the car as fast as it can go." What they should have said is, "I have enough intelligence not to do that." Some who were afraid of being considered a coward, and drove as fast as they could, were never able to drive again.

Some students have been suspended or expelled from schools because of doing something that they were dared to do. They had the option of remaining silent or of saying, "It's not worth it."

Some people have made investments that they could not afford because someone dared them to make them. An investment should be made rationally weighing all the known facts and data. Being dared does not provide as a reason for investing.

"I dare you to buy this expensive car," one whose self-interest it is that you should buy it might say to influence the buying of a car that one's rational mind would say, "This isn't for me."

Then there are bravado contests. Various members of a group might do things to show that they are the bravest. The winner is often the real loser.

"I have a principle. I never do something because someone dared me to do it," is a wise thing to say. I would write, "I dare you to say this if you are dared," but I will not because even this you should do because it makes sense and not because you have been dared.

*When I was a child, there was a boy whom the other children knew they could get to do almost anything if they dared him. There was the time that he pulled the school's fire alarm because of a dare. A different time the other students dared him to steal a copy of an upcoming test and he got caught. He felt that the other children all looked up to him as being brave. Instead they really looked at him as a weakling who could be easily manipulated. If he would have realized their true reactions, he would have saved himself from getting into trouble so frequently.*

*I read about a terrible bus accident. It was on the yearly trip of a high-school class. The passengers became friendly with the bus driver. As they were nearing the path of an oncoming train, a number of the kids who liked thrills challenged the bus driver, "Let's see if you have the guts to race the train to the intersection." Unfortunately the driver tried to impress the kids with his daring. The train won the race and the toll of deaths and injuries were high. How much braver it would have been for the bus driver to have given those children a lesson in safe driving.*

# 69

# CONDITION YOUR BRAIN

Right before you fall asleep at night, your brain is more open than usual to be programmed and conditioned. The suggestions you give your brain when you are in this state will have a more powerful effect than usual. Here is a sample of what you might want to tell your brain as you condition yourself. You might find it beneficial to make a tape of these messages and listen to the tape as you are falling asleep.

"I am grateful for the gift of courage that I already have. And now I am going to allow myself to be open to receiving even more courage.

"I will remember moments of courage that I experienced today. These moments add up with the moments of courage that I have experienced from the day I was born until now. And they will be added to the courage that I will experience tomorrow and in the future.

"If I experienced any lack of courage today, as I sleep my brain will rewrite those scenes and replay them the way I would have spoken and acted if I were to have had the highest levels of courage. Now these new scenes will be added to my inner resources.

"I am committed to use my courage to serve the Creator, to help other people, to continually grow and improve in every way, to accomplish and to begin again in any way that is needed.

"I am committed not to use my courage in any way that is against the will of my Creator, in any way that is harmful to other people, and in any way that is counterproductive or dangerous to myself.

"Tonight as I sleep, my brain will think of a situation in which I would benefit by having more courage. My brain will picture myself having that courage. I will see myself speaking the way I would speak with courage. This will always be in a way that is both self-respecting and respectful of others.

"My courage will be with humility and sensitivity. Tonight as I sleep my brain will become aware of any way that I speak or act that is an expression of arrogance and conceit and I will eliminate those patterns.

"I will use my courage to encourage others. I will focus on the specific needs of the people I encounter, and my own courage will enable me to share what I have learned with others.

"I will have the courage to acknowledge my mistakes, errors, and faults and with courage I will do all that I can to correct them.

"I will have the courage to forgive others, and I pray for the courage to ask forgiveness of anyone whom I have hurt in any way.

"Whether I will be aware of them or not, may I have dreams of courage. May these dreams enable me to accomplish my mission in this world. May these dreams enable me to cope well with any difficulties or adversities that arise in my life. May these dreams give me joy, kindness, and a strong will to do the will of my loving Father, and powerful King."

# 70

# HOLDING ON ANOTHER MINUTE

A famous general once said, "Courage is fear holding on another minute." We live a minute at a time. Some situations are so difficult that if we envision having courage for months or even weeks or even days at a time, we feel overwhelmed. But we can all hold on for another minute.

We need to plan for the future. We need to focus on the outcome of the things we say and do. But we still live only in the here and now, only in the present. To live with courage, we only need to do so one minute at a time.

The key to concentration is to focus our attention on the present. That is the only way we can pray properly. That is the only way we can study properly. That is the only way we can listen to what others are saying. And by focusing on the present and not what will be in fifteen minutes from now or an hour from now or a day from now or a week from now, we will be able to experience the courage we need for the needs of the moment.

Even if someone does not possess a self-image of being totally courageous, one can still allow oneself to be in a courageous state for a minute or two. And that is all it takes to live with courage. You only need to create this state one minute at a time.

By having courage for just one minute you will be able to continue adding to this state. The minutes add up to hours and the hours to days and the days to months. But this addition will compute automatically. You do not need to think about it. Your concern need only be for courage one minute at a time.

*I read of a person who hid on top of a tree to escape from enemies. He had to be totally still so they would not hear him. They remained in that vicinity the entire night and he did not have an idea of when they would leave. He held out for many hours. He was later asked how he felt during this terrifying experience.*

*"I only had to experience courage one minute at a time," he replied. "I didn't know how long I would have to stay where I was without food or water. I couldn't fall asleep no matter how long I would have to stay there. Not knowing the extent of time I would need to be in that tree, I kept telling myself that I only need to sustain my courage one minute at a time."*

*Ever since I read this, the idea of just holding on for another minute has been an inspiration to me. The situations when I need to hold on for another minute are usually not life threatening. I often visualize someone holding on to a rope on top of a cliff. He can't climb up and to fall would be disastrous. He is waiting for someone who knows he is in distress to pull him to the top. He can't stay there forever. But he can stay there one minute at a time. This has helped me in more mundane difficult situations.*

# 71.

# WHERE IS YOUR NEED?

Think about situations where you personally need greater courage. Depending on where a person is in life, these needs change. One day everything seem to be going wonderfully well, and the next day a challenge arises that calls for more courage than ever before. At times one feels overwhelmed with a situation, but circumstances change and one sees the light at the end of the tunnel.

After reading this book once, it is worthwhile to read it again focusing on your specific needs. Below is a partial list of various needs. Practice visualizing yourself having the necessary courage for all these situations. Courage enables you to think clearer about your wisest course of action in any given situation.

1. Acknowledging faults
2. Acknowledging you don't know
3. Admitting mistakes
4. Anger of others

5. Anxiety-provoking situations
6. Asking for advice
7. Asking for clarification
8. Asking for what you want
9. Asking forgiveness
10. Asking questions
11. Asking someone to stop speaking against another person
12. Beginning again
13. Being laughed at
14. Being stared at
15. Bouncing back after mistakes
16. Child rearing
17. Chronic pain
18. Collecting charity for others
19. Confronting people
20. Coping with difficult people
21. Correcting people
22. Criticism
23. Dangerous situations
24. Demands of others
25. Dilemmas
26. Disagreeing with others
27. Disasters
28. Doing good deeds when others are critical
29. Emotional risks
30. Facing death

31. Facing obstacles
32. Facing pain
33. Facing the unknown
34. Failure
35. Fearing rejection
36. Fears
37. Financial challenges
38. Forgiving
39. Handicaps
40. Hearing criticism
41. Illness
42. Illness of relatives and close friends
43. Insults
44. Interacting with an authority
45. Learning new skills
46. Legal problems
47. Loneliness
48. Losing
49. Marriage
50. Negotiating with a tough mediator
51. New environments
52. Offering help
53. Overcoming discouragement
54. Perplexing situations
55. Phobias
56. Remaining silent

57. Responsibilities
58. Returning a purchased item
59. Saying, "No."
60. Situations where there is loss of control
61. Speaking in public
62. Speaking to strangers
63. Stressful situations
64. Taking an unpopular position
65. Tension
66. To change one's mind
67. To express one's feelings
68. To forgive
69. To maintain one's position
70. To take emotional risks
71. To say, "I made a mistake."
72. To say, "I was wrong."
73. Unfamiliar situations
74. Unstable situations
75. Violence
76. Yelling of others

# 72.
# KING DAVID'S VERSES

King David was a model of courage. His spiritual awareness enabled him to cope with the most challenging of situations. His *Psalms* have served as inspiration in times of joy and in times of trouble and distress. Here is a selection of verses from *Psalms* that will help increase courage by repeating them regularly.

- "You, Hashem, are a shield for me, for my soul, and the One Who raises my head." (3:4)
- "I fear not the myriads of people deployed against me all around. Rise up, Hashem, save me, my G–d." (3:7-8)
- "Hashem will be a fortress for the oppressed, a fortress in times of distress. And those who know Your Name will trust in You, for You have not forsaken those who seek You, Hashem." (9:10-11)

Translation from "The Stone Edition Tanach"

- "I have set Hashem before me always; because He is at my right hand I shall not falter." (16:8)
- "You will make known to me the path of life, the fullness of joy in Your presence, the delights that are in Your right hand for eternity." (16:11)
- "Demonstrate clearly Your kindness, [You] Who saves with Your right hand those who seek refuge [in You] from those who arise [against them]. Guard me like the apple of the eye; shelter me in the shadow of Your wings." (17:7-8)
- "Hashem is My Rock, My Fortress and my Rescuer; my G–d, my Rock in Whom I take shelter, my Shield, and the Horn of my Salvation, my Stronghold." (18:3)
- "For it is You Who will light my lamp, Hashem, my G–d, illuminates my darkness." (18:29)
- "It is G–d Who girds me with strength." (18:33)
- "You have given me the shield of Your salvation; and Your right hand has sustained me." (18:36)
- "Hashem lives! Blessed is my Rock; and the G–d of my salvation is exalted." (18:47)
- "May Hashem answer you on the day of distress." (20:2)
- "Some with chariots, and some with horses; but we, in the Name of Hashem, our G–d, call out. They slumped and fell, but we arose and were invigorated; Hashem save! May the King answer us on the day we call." (20:8-10)
- "In You, our fathers trusted, they trusted and You delivered them." (22:5)

- "Hashem is my shepherd, I shall not lack." (23:1)
- "Though I walk in the valley overshadowed by death, I will fear no evil, for You are with me." (23:4)
- "My eyes are constantly toward Hashem, for He will remove my feet from the snare." (25:15)
- "Protect my soul and rescue me, let me not be ashamed, for I take refuge in You." (25:20)
- "Hashem is my light and my salvation, whom shall I fear? Hashem is my life's strength, whom shall I dread?" (27:1)
- "Though an army would besiege me, my heart would not fear; though war would arise against me, in this I trust. One thing I asked of Hashem, that shall I seek: Would that I dwell in the House of Hashem all the days of my life, to behold the sweetness of Hashem and to contemplate in His Sanctuary." (27:3-4)
- "Hope to Hashem; strengthen yourself and He will give you courage, and hope to Hashem." (27:14)
- "Hashem is my strength and my shield, in Him my heart trusted and I was helped; and My heart exulted, with my song I praise Him." (28:7)
- "Hear, Hashem, and favor me; Hashem, be my Helper!" (30:11)
- "You are my Rock and my fortress, for your Name's sake guide me and lead me." (31:4)
- "Be strong, and let your hearts take courage, all who wait longingly for Hashem." (31:25)

- "Kindness surrounds the one who trusts in Hashem." (32:10)
- "Behold, the eye of Hashem is on those who fear Him, upon those who await His kindness. To rescue their soul from death, and to sustain them in famine. Our soul longed for Hashem; He is our help and our shield." (33:18-20)
- "I sought out Hashem, and He answered me, and from all my terrors He delivered me." (34:5)
- "This poor man calls and Hashem hears, and from all his troubles He saves him." (34:7)
- "How precious is Your kindness, O G–d! Mankind takes refuge in the shelter of Your wings." (36:8)
- "By Your light, may we see light." (36:10)
- "The salvation of the righteous is from Hashem, their Might in time of distress. Hashem helped them and caused them to escape; He will cause them to escape from the wicked and He will save them, for they took refuge in Him." (37:39-40)
- "I have greatly hoped for Hashem; He inclined to me, and heard my cry." (40:2)
- "Praiseworthy is the man who has made Hashem his trust, and turned not to the arrogant, and to strayers after falsehood."(40:5)
- "You, Hashem, do not withhold Your mercy from me; may Your kindness and Your truth always protect me." (40:12)
- "May it be Your will, Hashem, to rescue me; Hashem, hasten to my assistance." (40:14)

- "Why are you downcast, my soul, and why are you disturbed on my account? Hope to G–d! For I shall yet thank Him for the salvations of my countenance and because He is my G–d." (42:12)
- "G–d is a refuge and strength for us, a help in distress, very accessible. Therefore, we shall not be afraid when the earth is transformed, and at mountains' collapse in the heart of the seas." (46:2-3)
- "Create a pure heart for me, O G–d, and a steadfast spirit renew within me. Cast me not away from Your presence, and take not Your Holy Spirit from me. Restore to me the joy of Your salvation, and with a generous spirit sustain me." (51:12-14)
- "Cast upon Hashem your burden and He will sustain you." (55:23)
- "In G–d I have trusted, I shall not fear." (56:12)
- "For You have been a refuge for me, a tower of strength in the face of the enemy." (61:4)
- "For G–d alone my soul waits silently, from Him comes my salvation. He alone is my Rock and my Salvation." (62:2-3)
- "Trust in Him at every moment." (62:9)
- "Praiseworthy is the man whose strength is in You, those whose hearts focus on upward paths." (84:6)
- "Whoever sits in the refuge of the Most High, he shall dwell in the [protective] shade of the A-mighty. I will say of

Hashem, [He is] my refuge and my fortress, my G–d, I will trust in Him." (91:1-2)

- "I raise my eyes upon the mountains. Whence will come my help? My help is from Hashem, Maker of heaven and earth." (121:1-2)
- "Hashem is close to all who call upon Him, to all who call upon Him sincerely." (145:18)